The Big Story

Michael Cohen

Special thanks to my wife Melanie Lotfali, for believing in this creative process and turning ideas into reality.

v1.0 - Many thanks to those who have provided invaluable feedback to this book's inception: Ms PenelopeTaylor, Dr Shakib Shahidian, Ms Amica Gordon, Ms Jessica Vahdat, Mr Hessam Shahidi.

v1.2 - Thanks to Mr Robin Mihrshahi for improving the scientific rigor of the book. Thanks to Mr Todd Smith at ISGP for suggestions and encouragement.

Version 2.0 - 2017

ISBN 978-0-9874934-1-5

www.michelangela.com.au

INTRODUCTION

This is the first book in the ***Reflections on Reality*** series.

The Big Story explains the way in which the purposeful process of evolution, which has brought human beings into existence, has taken place gradually over time and space.

The Bahá'í Faith, which seeks unity within the diversity of humanity, offers guidance to reveal the false dichotomy pitting the concepts of evolution and creation against each other.

Science and religion are shown to be two windows on one reality, two knowledge systems that when properly understood, function as one cohesive whole for the advancement and wellbeing of humanity.

THE BIG STORY

IN THE BEGINNING

Human knowledge and understanding is constantly evolving. The knowledge available now is much more advanced than that which was available even a generation ago. It is impossible to imagine the knowledge and understanding which will be gained about human beings and the universe in the years ahead.

It is currently thought that matter (that is, everything in the physical universe) is made up of molecules. Molecules are made from atoms. Atoms are made up of protons, neutrons and electrons, and these are made from quarks. Some scientists believe that quarks are made from tiny vibrations of energy. And all of this started with a BANG!

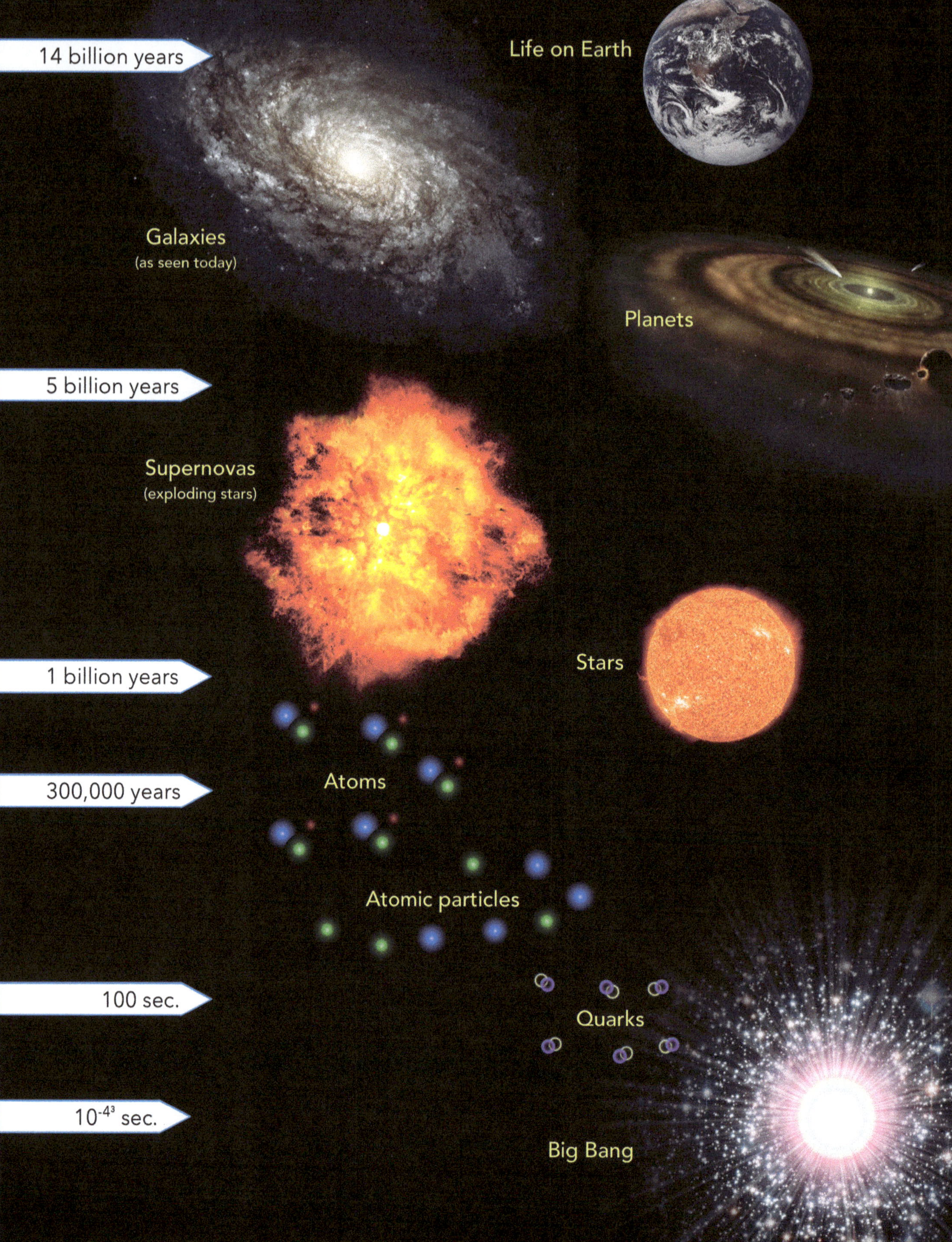
14 billion years
Life on Earth
Galaxies
(as seen today)
Planets
5 billion years
Supernovas
(exploding stars)
1 billion years
Stars
300,000 years
Atoms
Atomic particles
100 sec.
Quarks
10^{-43} sec.
Big Bang

Formation of the Universe

Scientists currently believe that nearly fourteen billion years ago, what we now call the universe, exploded from an infinitesimal point to the size of a galaxy in less than a trillion trillionth of a second. As the energy spread over a vast volume the smallest building blocks of matter began to emerge.

Quarks emerged from unknown energetic or material constituents and formed subatomic particles: protons, neutrons and electrons. Subatomic particles are the building blocks of atoms. The first atom to form was the simplest and lightest atom: Hydrogen. Hydrogen atoms have one proton, one neutron, and one electron.

Formation of Stars

Hydrogen atoms were attracted to each other through the force of gravity. They were pulled closer and closer to each other until they formed vast clouds. The clouds condensed further and a nucleus was formed. Within this nucleus the heat and pressure caused an atomic reaction called fusion. That is, two hydrogen atoms joined together under immense pressure and heat creating a new heavier atom: Helium. Helium is heavier because it has two protons, two neutrons, and two electrons. Fusion reactions not only created helium, but also produced heat and light - known as a star. The sun is just one of those stars.

Billions of stars formed. Some were huge. Some were small. Some burned quickly, and some slowly. The stars were attracted to each other by gravity. Due to gravity, the stars formed into patterns of slowly swirling spirals, called spiral galaxies.

When the stars which were quick to burn exploded at the end of their life, other heavier atoms like oxygen and iron were formed within the intense pressures of the explosion. These heavier atoms contributed to the dust clouds from which the planets of the solar system were formed. Thus, planets such as Earth were made from the remains of exploding stars. We are stardust.

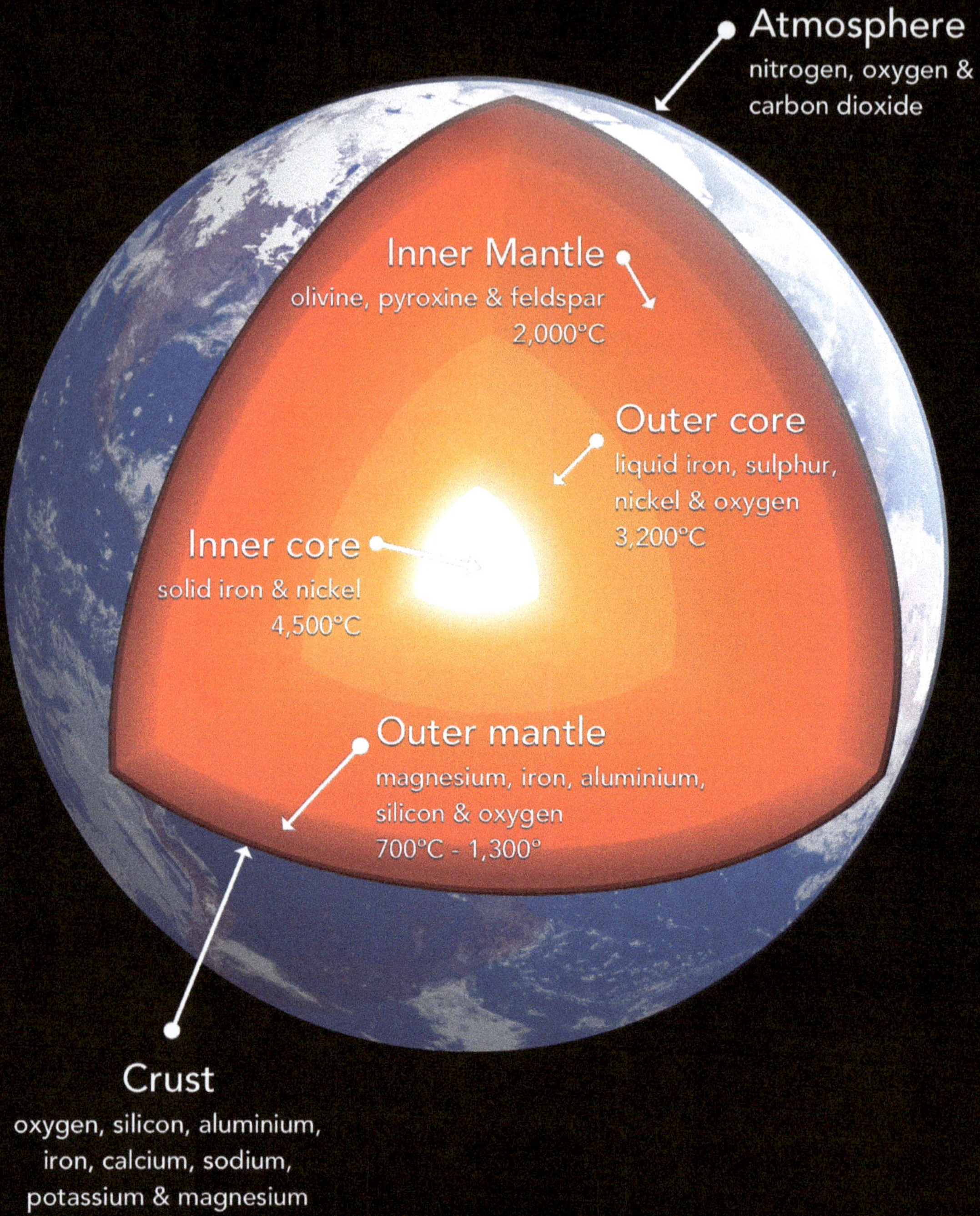

Atmosphere

nitrogen, oxygen &
carbon dioxide

Inner Mantle

olivine, pyroxine & feldspar
2,000°C

Outer core

liquid iron, sulphur,
nickel & oxygen
3,200°C

Inner core

solid iron & nickel
4,500°C

Outer mantle

magnesium, iron, aluminium,
silicon & oxygen
700°C - 1,300°

Crust

oxygen, silicon, aluminium,
iron, calcium, sodium,
potassium & magnesium

Formation of Earth

Due to gravity, the cloud of dust rotating around the sun coalesced into balls of spinning matter which formed into the planets of the solar system.

Exactly how this process ensued is debatable. However, approximately 4.5 billion years ago, smaller particles coalesced into bigger particles, leading to the clumping of matter. Dense material sank to the center and the lighter material formed the molten surface.

As the Earth cooled over time, it formed a crust and a primitive atmosphere. The earth's atmosphere is the envelope of gases surrounding it. Active volcanoes spewed out gases like water vapor, carbon dioxide, and ammonia.

It is possible that collisions with comets resulted in the deposit of much of the Earth's water. Due to the ideal temperature of the Earth, most of this water remained on the surface to form the seas.

Earth

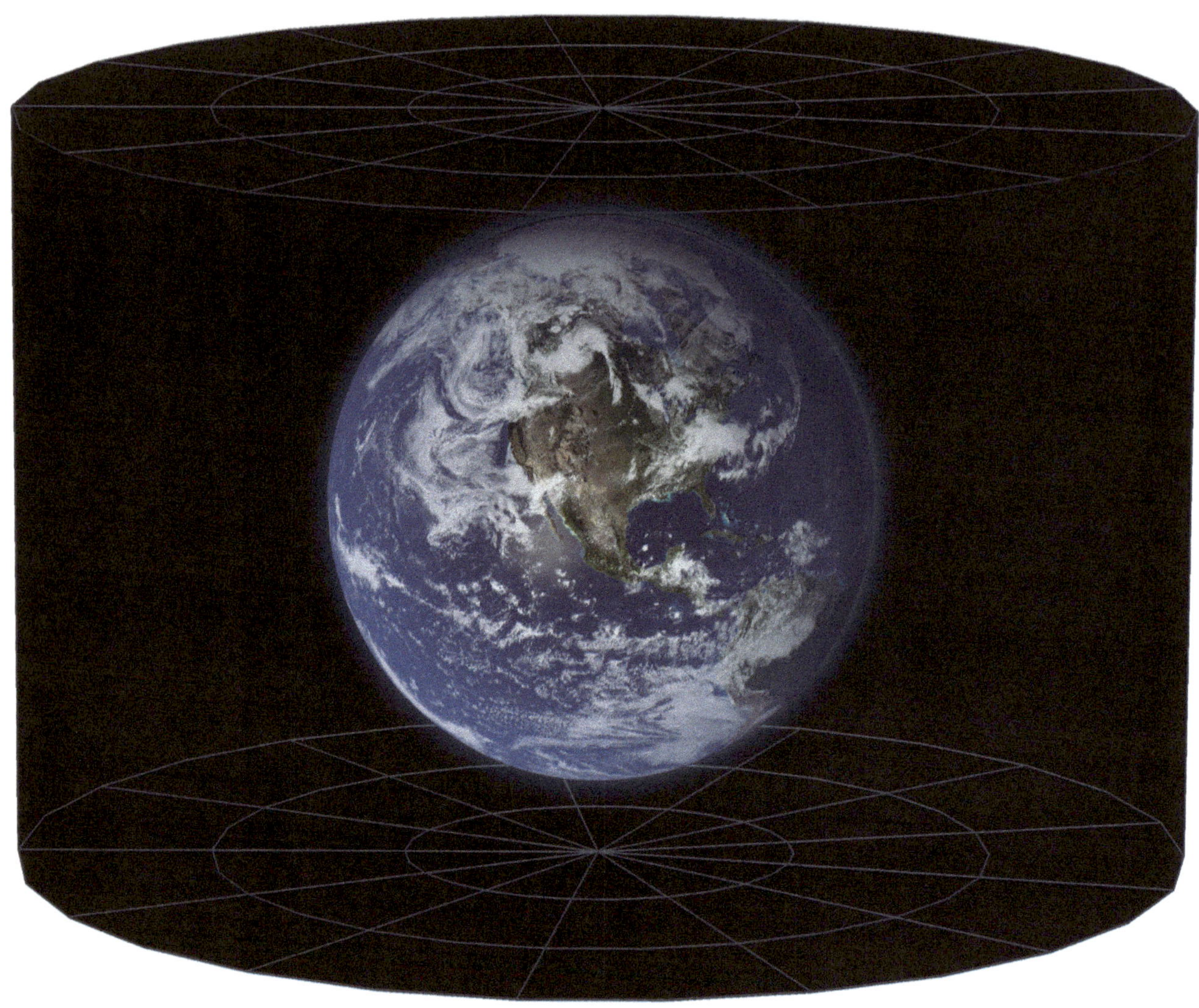

The circumference of Earth is 40,000 km (25,000 miles). That is, approximately 45 hours by Boeing jet aircraft, or 33 hours at the speed of sound, or 0.13 seconds at the speed of light.

Solar System

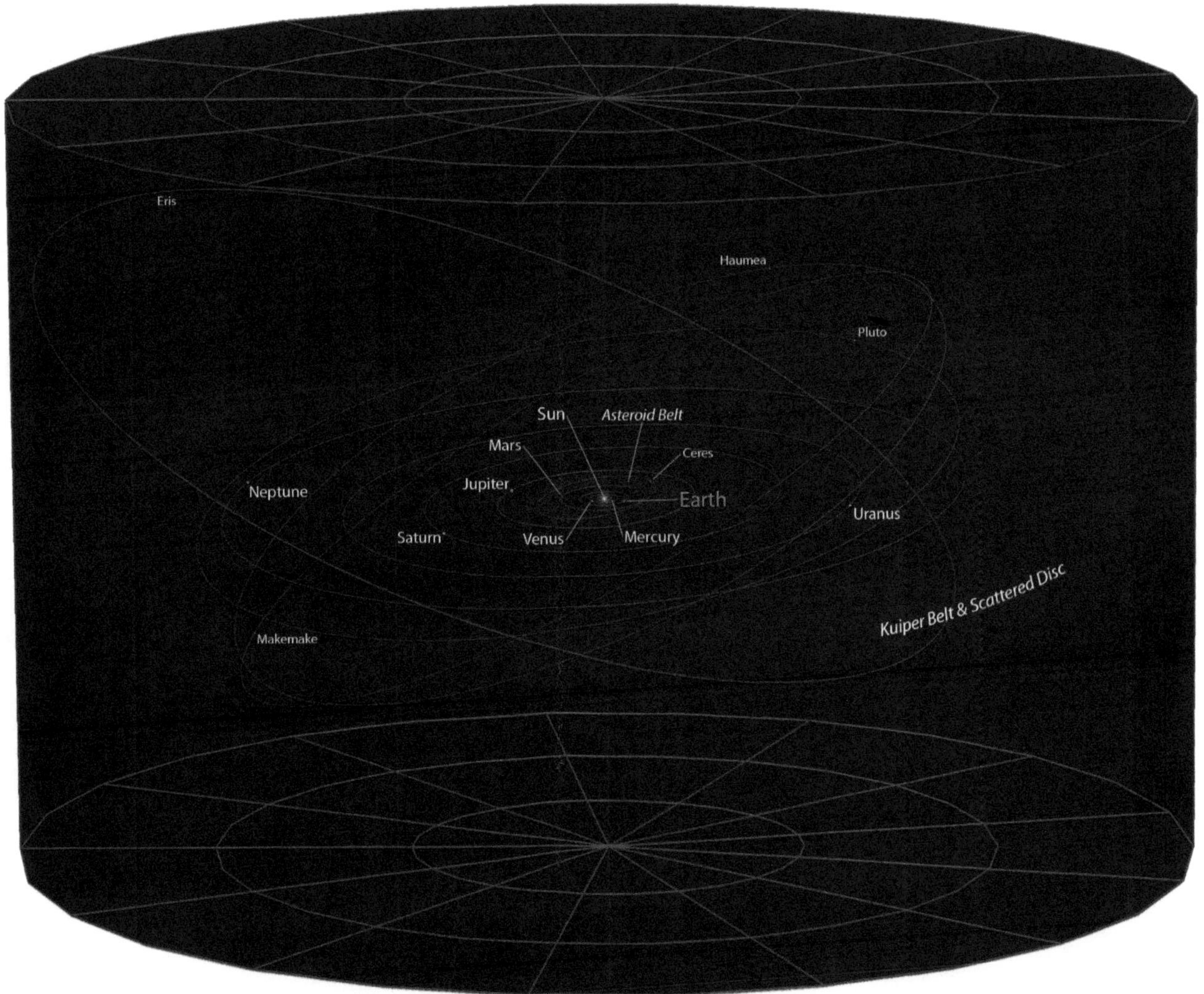

The solar system comprises the sun and eight planets - Mercury, Venus, Earth, Mars, Jupiter, Saturn, Neptune & Uranus. The approximate radius (distance from center) of the solar system is 13 billion kilometers (8 billion miles), or 12 hours at the speed of light.

Solar Interstellar Neighborhood

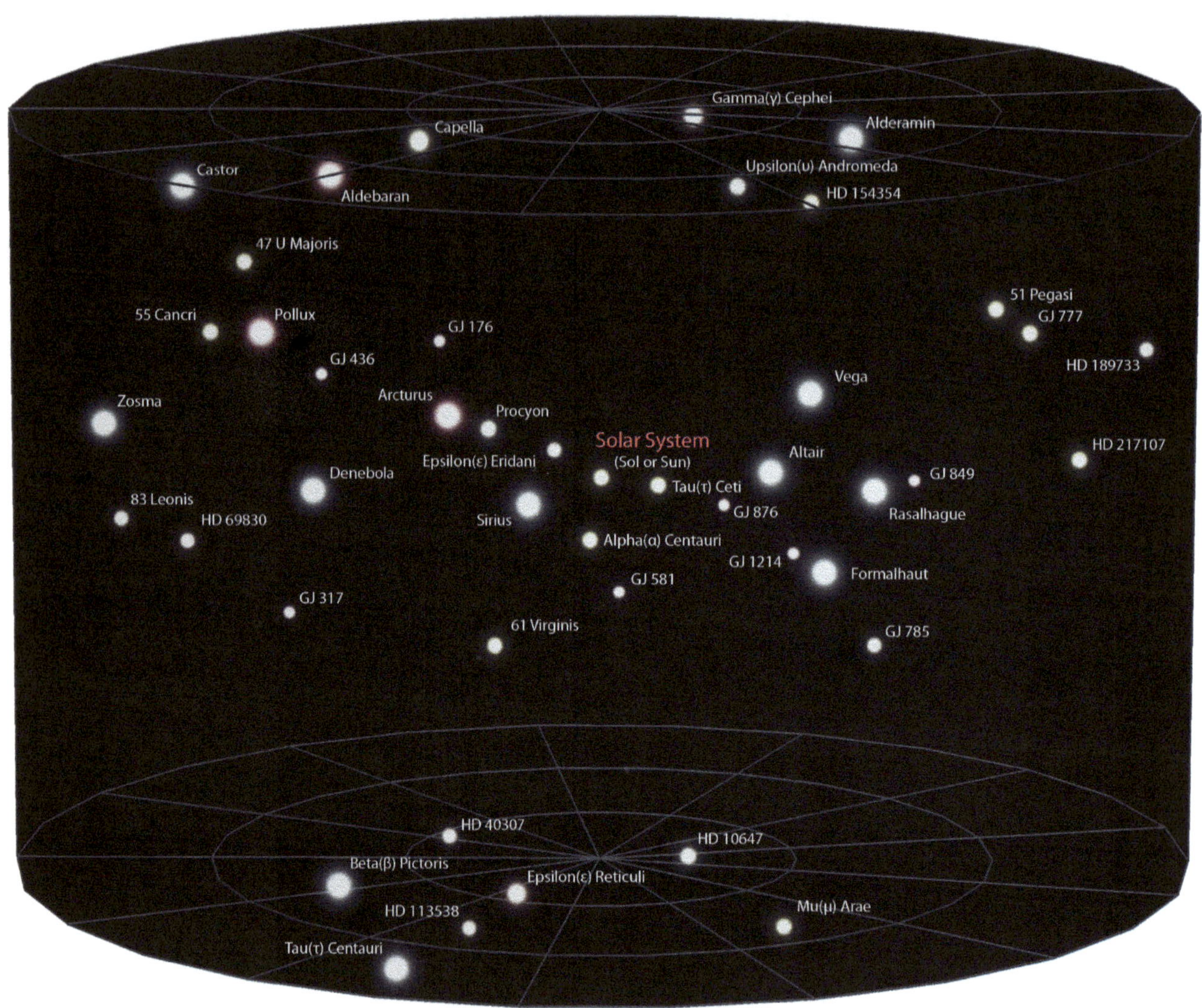

The Solar Interstellar Neighborhood is made up of the cluster of stars nearest to Earth's sun. The distance to the nearest star, Alpha Centauri, is 4.2 years at the speed of light, 4.2 light years.

Milky Way Galaxy

The Milky Way Galaxy is the name of the spiral galaxy of stars in which Earth is located. The diameter of the Milky Way Galaxy is approximately 120,000 light years. It contains approximately 200 billion stars.

Local Galactic Group

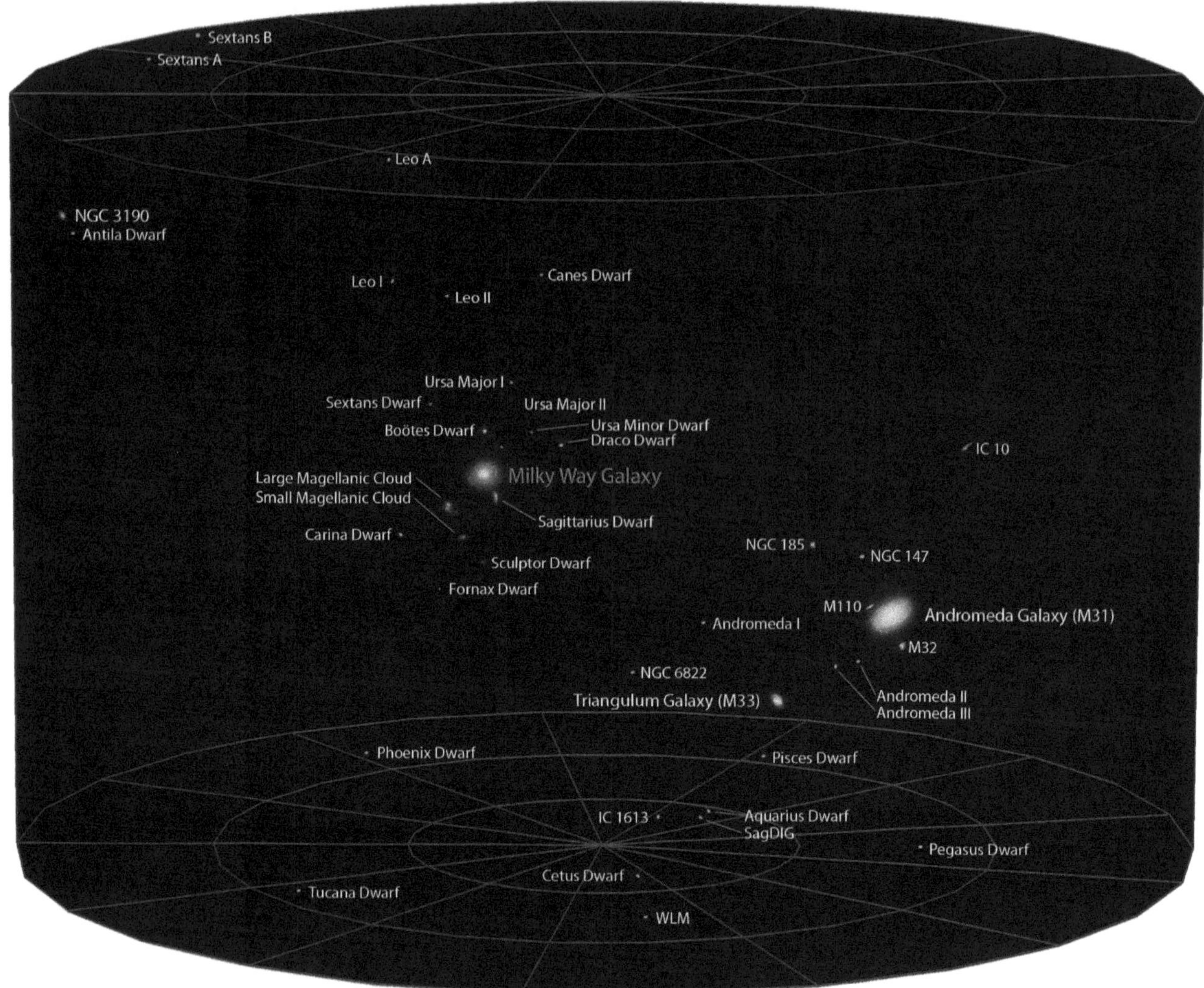

The Local Galactic Group is a collection of galaxies near the Milky Way Galaxy consisting of 54 galaxies. The diameter of the Local Galactic Group is 10 million light years.

Laniakea Supercluster

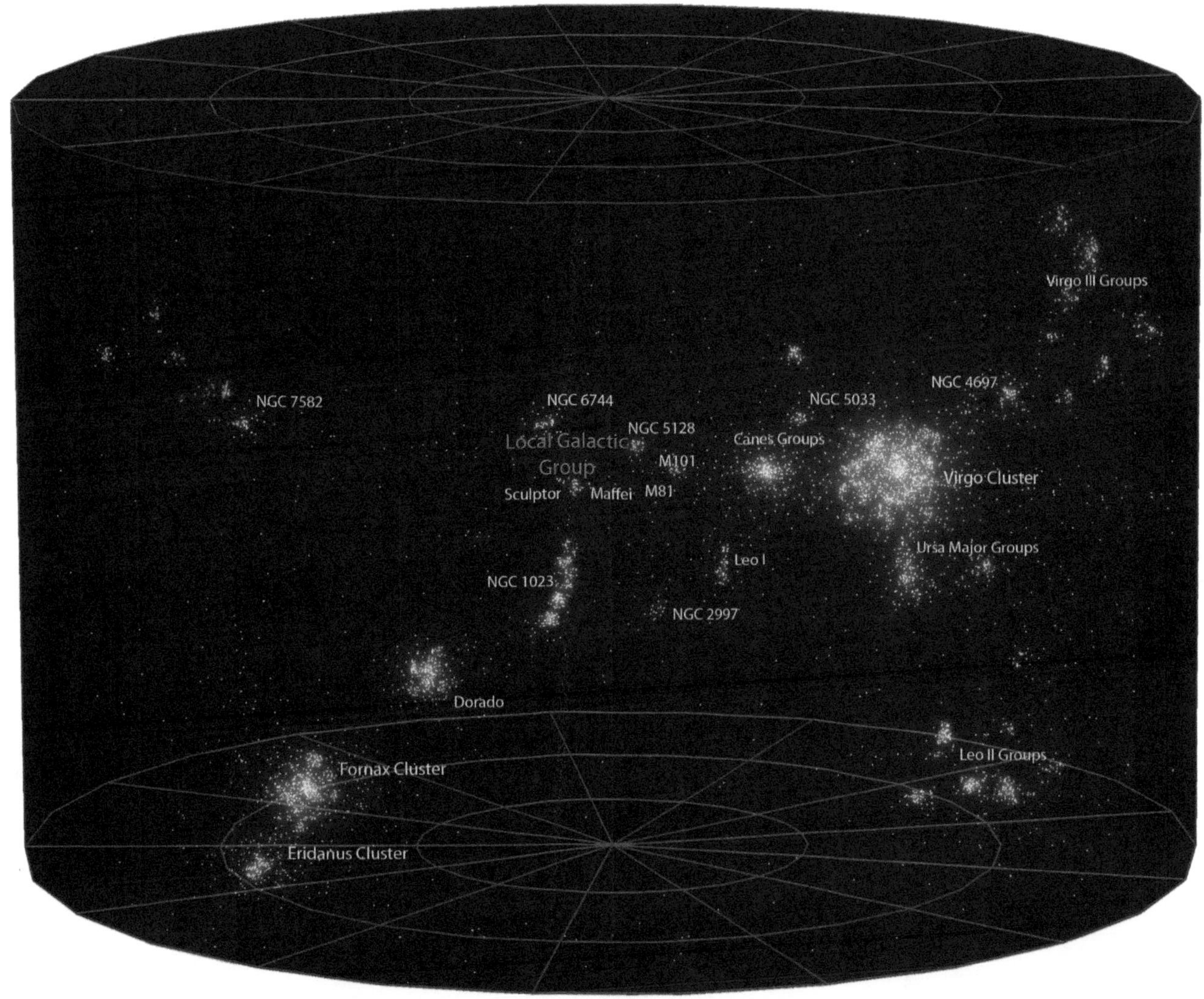

The Laniakea Supercluster is a large cluster of galaxies separated from other clusters in the universe. One of millions in the universe. The diameter of Laniakea Supercluster is 520 million light years. The above image is the Virgo Supercluster, re-identified in 2014 as a portion of the Laniakea Supercluster.

Local Superclusters

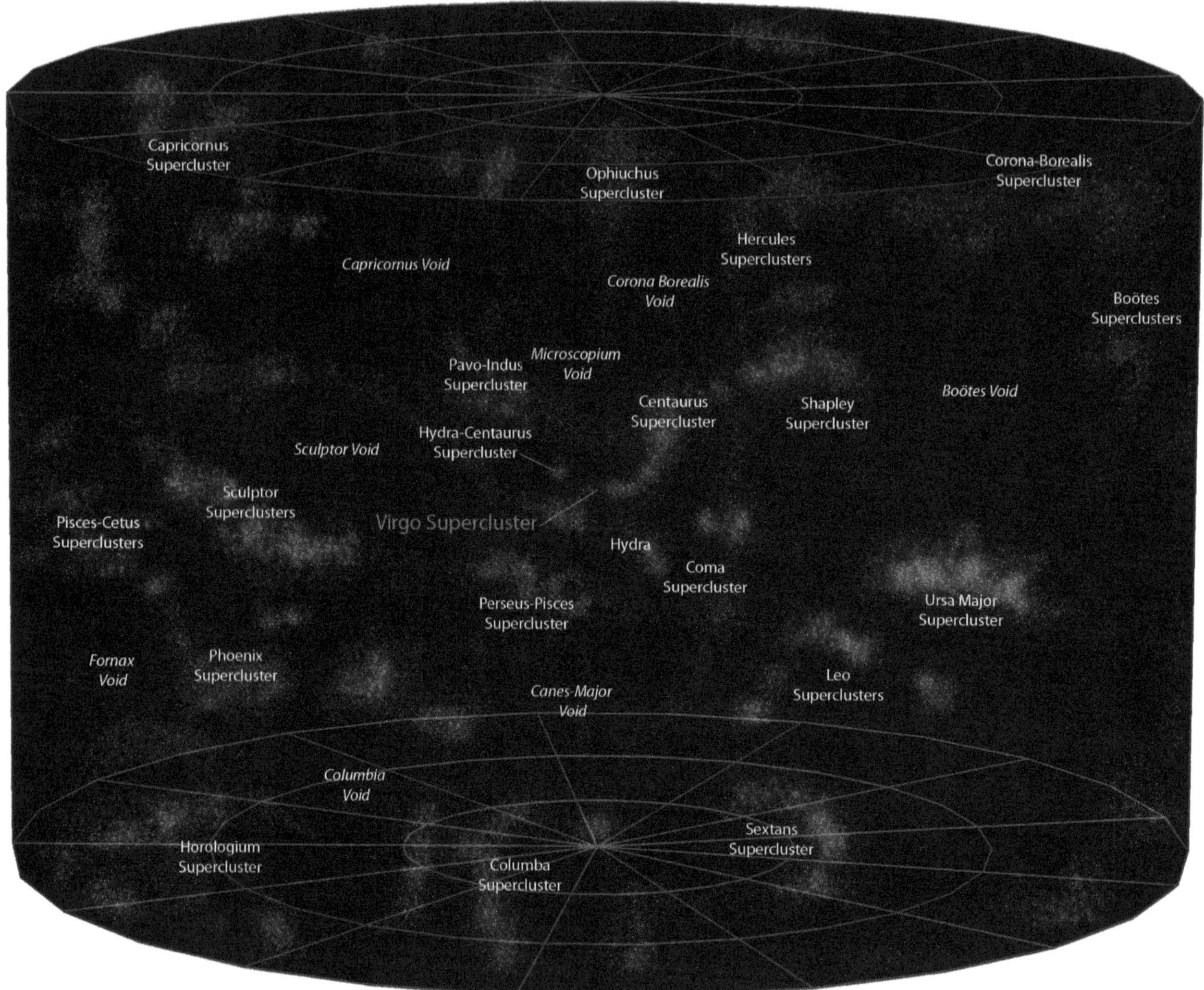

The Local Supercluster is a collection of superclusters in the known universe. The diameter of the Local Supercluster is one billion light years.

Observable Universe

The observable universe is everything which exists from the Big Bang. It comprises approximately 170 billion galaxies, 34 sextillion (34,000,000,000,000,000,000,000) stars. The diameter of the observable universe is 93 billion light years.

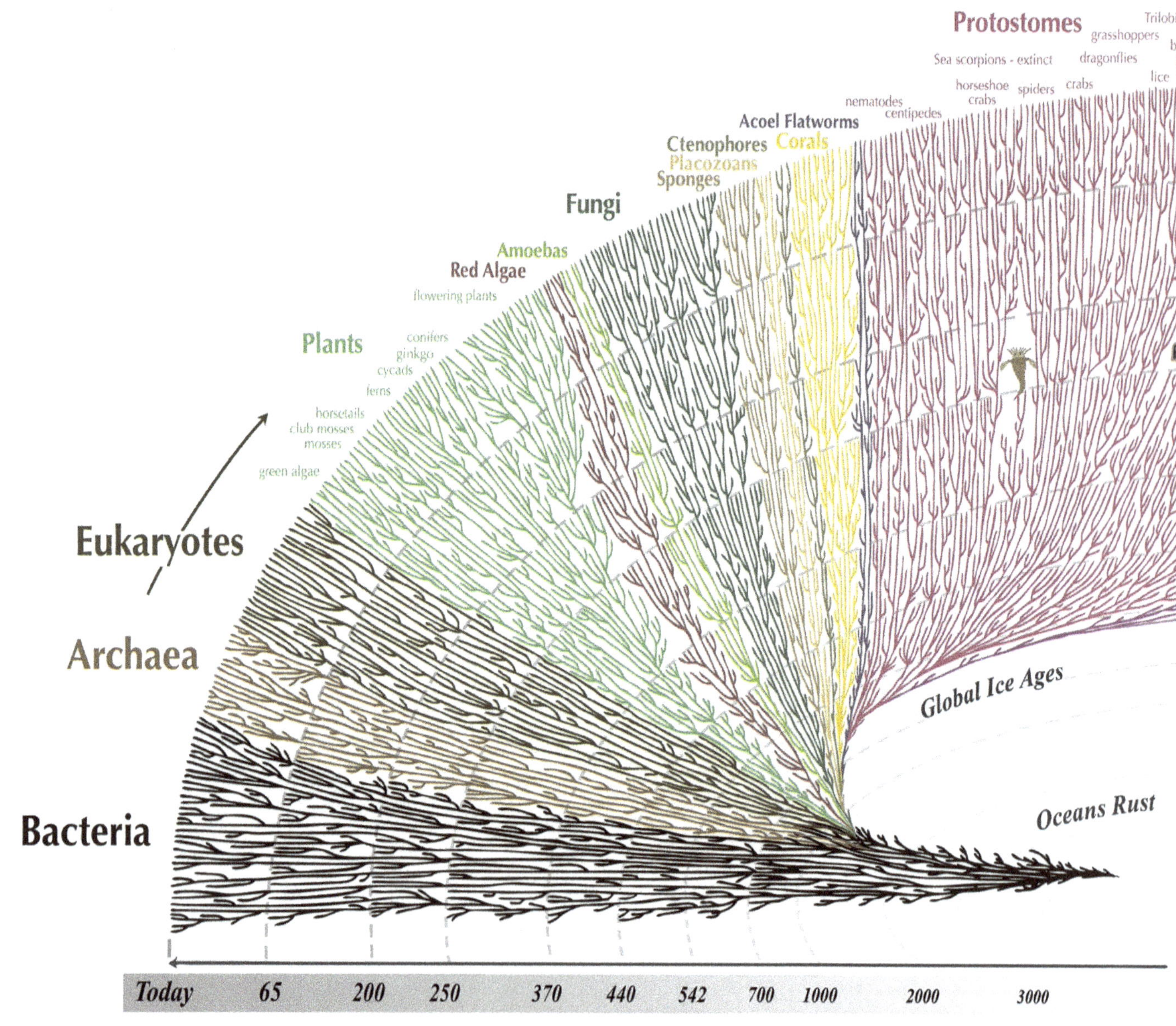

Millions of Years Ago

EVOLUTION

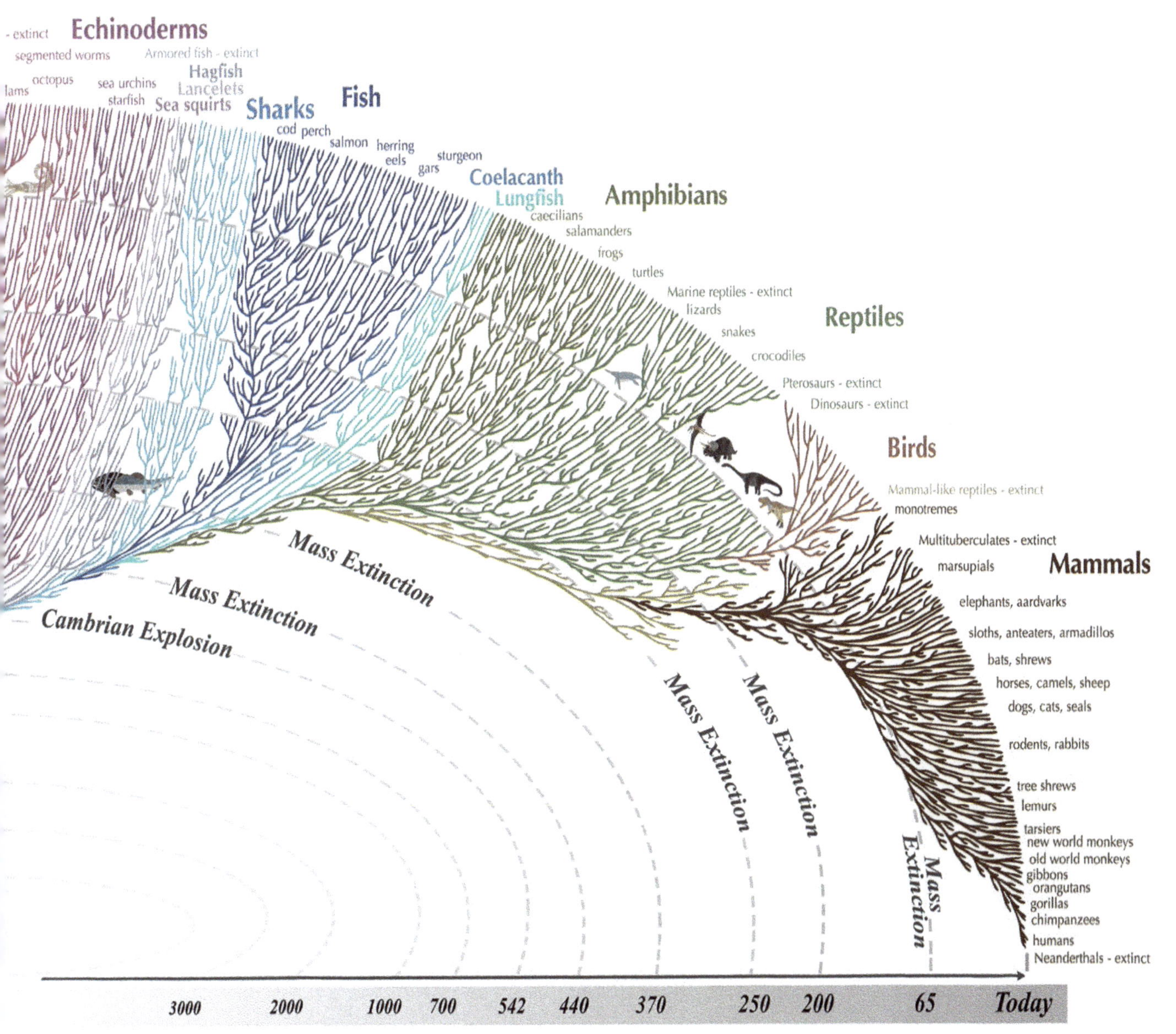

Millions of Years Ago

MESOZOIC ERA
251 MILLION YEARS AGO
200 MY AGO
TRIASSIC PERIOD
JURASSIC PERIOD
CRETACEOUS PERIOD
65 MILLION YEARS AGO
TERTIARY PERIOD
Paleocene Epoch
Eocene Epoch
Oligocene Epoch
Miocene Epoch
Pliocene Epoch
Pleistocene Epoch
Holocene Epoch
TERTIARY PERIOD
QUATERNARY PERIOD
CENOZOIC ERA
PALEOZOIC ERA
CAMBRIAN PERIOD
ORDOVICIAN PERIOD
SILURIAN PERIOD
DEVONIAN PERIOD
MISSISSIPPIAN PERIOD
PENNSYLVANIAN PERIOD
PERMIAN PERIOD
PRECAMBRIAN
1 BILLION YEARS AGO
2 BILLION YEARS AGO
3 BILLION YEARS AGO EARLIEST ORGANIC STRUCTURES
4.5 BILLION YEARS AGO

Evolution of Life

Evolution is the change in the inherited characteristics of biological organisms over many generations. Evolutionary processes give rise to diversity at every level of biological organization, including species, individual organisms, and molecules.

Evolution is a process which leads to greater diversity and inter-dependency of all living things. Successful organisms which adapt to changing environments are the ones to survive. For example: tortoises with longer necks can reach more leafy food in times of drought; insects which are camouflaged have less chance of being eaten; organisms which have more offspring increase their chance of survival; organisms which are quicker, stronger, or more intelligent have better survival rates than those which are more vulnerable.

Over millions of years life forms have increased in complexity. This complexity is awe-inspiring in its beauty and detail, and intriguing in its inter-dependency.

Water has properties which are not predictable from its composition of hydrogen and oxygen. Both hydrogen and oxygen by themselves are very reactive. Both burn intensely and are dangerous to store. Oxygen can rust many metals. But when they combine to form water they become very benign, passive, inert, stable, and the perfect molecule to support life. In fact human adults are 60% water and human babies are almost 80% water!

Nucleic Acids

From simple ingredients of carbon, hydrogen, nitrogen and oxygen comes the formation of nucleotides, the building blocks of essential nucleic acids such as DNA (Deoxyribonucleic acid) and RNA (Ribonucleic acid). Nucleic acids have functionality to replicate themselves.

Nucleotides such as RNA and DNA can be synthesized in the laboratory from constituent materials. These constituent materials have also been found in meteorites, indicating that the building blocks of life are pervasive throughout the universe. These molecules may have formed at the time when the Earth was no more than dust rotating around the Sun.

On the earth, the combination of watery environments and heat seeping through the crust provided ideal conditions for further chemical reactions and increased complexity. It is believed that these environments, home to the macromolecules for all forms of life (nucleic acids, proteins, fats, and sugars), is where life on Earth began.

The oldest physical traces of biological life on Earth date back 4.1 billion years. The natural process of life arising from non-living matter is known as abiogenesis.

Simple Cells

Approximately 3.9 billion years ago the first protocells formed. Protocells are self-organized, ordered, spherical collections of water-resistant molecules. These cells are believed to be the precursors of the single cell organisms prokaryotes and bacteria. These cells contained compartmentalized organelles which performed specific functions for the cell such as the generation of energy, reproduction, movement, communication, and connection to other cells.

An example of a simple cell is a bacterial cell. Bacteria provide essential functions for all life on Earth. Bacteria can live in colonies. They are aware of their environment and communicate with other organisms and their host. Within the human body there are ten times more bacterial cells than human-body cells!

Bacteria called cyanobacteria (blue-green algae) produced most of the oxygen in Earth's atmosphere about 2.4 billion years ago. The creation of oxygen in Earth's atmosphere allowed for the eventual growth of plants, the oxygenation of the sea, and ultimately for the evolution of more complex life.

Please note that this diagram is a simplistic linear representation of what is actually a vast and complex evolutionary tree.

Evolution of Plants

From the simple blue-green algae cyanobacteria which first inhabited Earth's waters, multi-cellular organisms evolved. Multi-cellular means there are many cells all working together in an organism. Plants are examples of multi-cellular organisms. At first the only plants on Earth were found in the sea.

About 500 million years ago plants that could live outside of the sea started to flourish. Over hundreds of millions of years, these plants developed in complexity. Describing the process in the most simple terms, it can be said that algae evolved to form mosses which developed into ferns. Ferns became conifers and these developed into flowering plants and grains.

As plants evolved, the ways in which they reproduced also became more complex and varied. Only recently in the evolutionary timescale, have plants used spores, seeds, and flowers to reproduce.

Plants (and some bacteria) are able to transform the energy from the sun into sugars. This process is called photosynthesis. It relies on a molecule called chlorophyll. It is chlorophyll which makes plants green. These sugars can then be used as energy to support growth. Leaf-eating animals and insects use plant sugars for their own energy and growth.

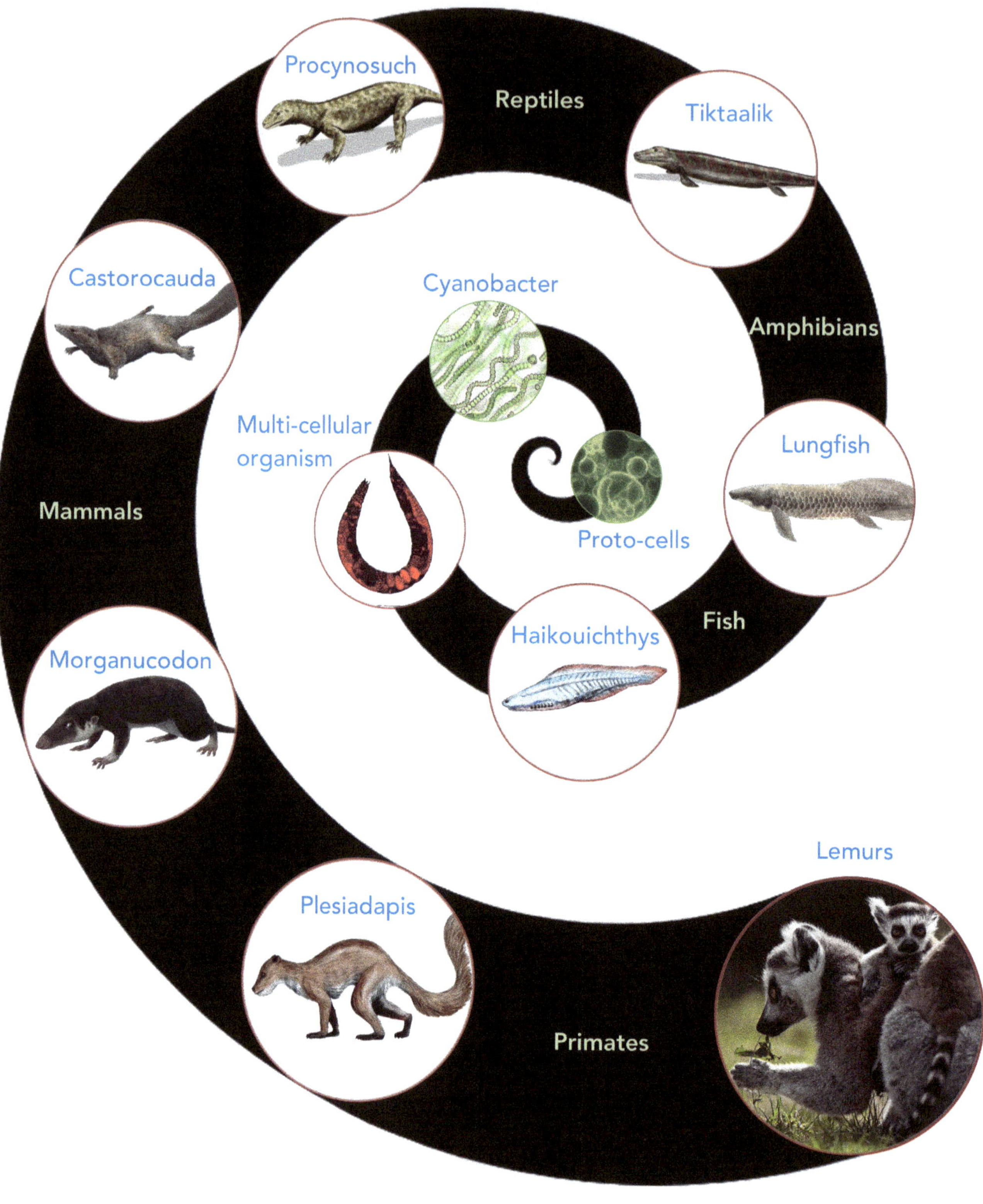

Please note that this diagram is a simplistic linear representation of what is actually a vast and complex evolutionary tree.

Evolution of Mammals

Animals first evolved from simple long multi-cellular organisms, arranged in repeating segments. These segments were like repeating segments of a worm, connected by a nervous system (a communication system for the body). To help keep the organism rigid and strong a skeleton evolved with long connecting muscles to assist with movement.

The inner skeleton defined the organism's body shape. These animals were called vertebrates. Some vertebrates continued to live in the sea. These developed into animals like fish and sharks. Other vertebrates further evolved and adapted to life outside of the sea. Once again, describing the process in the most simple terms, it can be said that fish evolved into amphibians and then into reptiles. As evolution continued, reptiles branched into marsupials, then into mammals.

Mammals emerged about 120 million years ago. Mammals are animals that grow their young in a womb, feed their babies with milk from their own bodies, and have fur. Mammals have a neocortex which is a part of the brain not found in earlier organisms. This allows for greater sense processing, spatial reasoning, conscious thought and complex communication. Examples of mammals include dogs, cats and primates (like lemurs and monkeys).

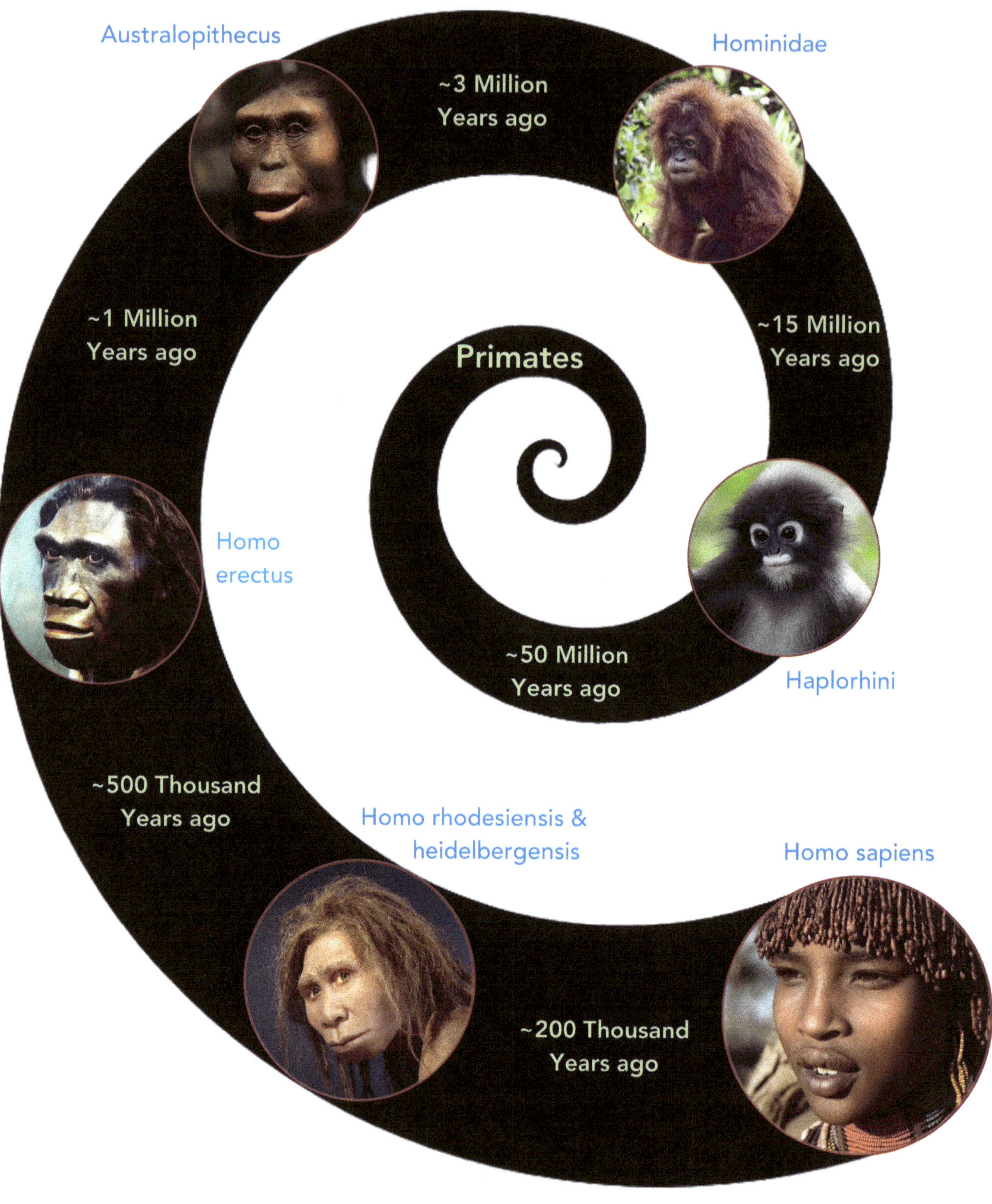

Please note that this diagram is a simplistic linear representation of what is actually a vast and complex evolutionary tree.

Evolution of Humans

The most adaptable and intelligent of the primates evolved into monkeys and apes. Human beings have a common ancestor with apes and monkeys like chimpanzees. This common ancestor existed approximately seven million years ago. Homo Sapiens (current human beings) evolved about 200,000 years ago. Humans were physically distinguished from monkeys by the way they walked on two legs and by the size of the brain.

There are several theories seeking to explain the development of intelligence in humans. One theory emphasizes the changes in social grouping, where the emergence of larger and more complex social groups may have contributed to an increase in intelligence.

Another theory emphasizes the impact of changes in the environment. This necessitated adaptation and the development of new skills. Two factors that contributed to change in the environment of early humans included global climate change, such as ice ages, and growing human populations. As human populations increased, groups were forced to move into new land areas, learn new skills and master their new environment.

An alternative explanation, which is supported by teachings of the Baha'i Faith, suggests that the process of evolution, while seemingly driven by chance and circumstance, has always contained the potential for the development of human intelligence. Thus it can be said that human intelligence was inevitable, and its appearance required only opportunity, which emerged over time.

SOCIETY

A human society is a social grouping sharing the same territory, following the same leaders and obeying the same rules. Within a society, people are connected through various relationships including familial, religious, political and economic relationships.

It is believed that Homo Sapiens migrated from Africa at least 60,000 years ago. They first migrated into Asia, then Australasia, then the Americas. Throughout this time, humans gathered in ever-larger groups.

Years Ago	Community	People
100,000–10,000	Tribes	10s–100s
10,000–5,000	Villages	100s–1,000s
5,000–4,000	Chiefdoms	1,000s–10,000s
4,000–3,000	States	10,000s–100,000s
3,000–today	Empires & Nations	100,000s–1,000,000s

Early societies were made up of bands of hunter-gatherers. These bands then evolved into nomadic tribes. Over time, some of these nomadic tribes established fixed homes and farms for growing food. Diverse cultures and communities were established. This led to the unification of people in more and more complex social arrangements.

Today on Earth there are almost 6,000 languages.
All languages have the capacity to express a similar set of complex ideas.

200,000 years ago

Language evolved over the last 200,000 years. Changes in the human brain, throat, lips and vocal chords were important for the development of language. As language evolved it allowed humans to communicate and think in more complex ways.

50,000 years ago

Art, music, cooking, games, self-ornamentation, trade, and burial rites were evident among humans about 50,000 years ago. These expressions of creativity are the signs of developing culture.

20,000 years ago

Hunter-gatherer societies formed about 20,000 years ago. In these societies people lived by hunting animals and collecting plant foods. They used tools such as bows, spears and stone axes for hunting, and stone knives and digging sticks for gathering. Dogs were engaged to help hunt and protect.

12,000 years ago

Farming societies formed around 12,000 years ago. Humans started to gather and replant grass seeds such as wheat, rice and barley. In gardens, potatoes, chickpeas, beans and figs were grown. People started to live in fixed dwellings made from mud and stone. About 8,000 years ago people domesticated wild animals such as sheep and goats for food and milk.

An early accounting record made of clay.

5,000 years ago

About 5,000 years ago some early civilizations began to create industries of metalwork, pottery, artwork, and trade. In many societies people were organized into social classes. Social classes included a ruling-class elite, middle-class traders, and lower-class workers.

Initially, bartering was used for the trade of items and services, but as society became complex, tokens or money were used. Money was first used in Mesopotamia about 5,000 years ago. Societies in the Americas, Asia, Africa and Australia used shell money – often cowry shells. It is thought by modern scholars that stamped coins were first used around 2,600 years ago.

During the same period writing was invented. As societies grew in size, people needed a means to send information, maintain financial accounts, and keep historical records. About 5,000 years ago, the complexity of trade and administration outgrew human memory. Writing was a dependable method of recording events.

Also around 5,000 years ago, the use of plants, animal parts and minerals for healing, began to be known as 'medicine'. In many cases these materials were used in healing rituals. An Egyptian by the name of Imhotep who lived 5,000 years ago may have been the first doctor known to history.

In the parts of the world directly impacted by the Industrial Revolution, chronic hunger and malnutrition were the norm for the majority of the population. Life expectancy was about 35 years. The use of child labor was rampant and many children were forced to work for 20% of an adult male's wage. Children as young as four were employed. Beatings and long hours were common. Some child coal miners worked from 4am until 5pm. Conditions were dangerous. Many children were killed when they dozed off and fell into the path of the mining carts, while others died from gas explosions.

3,000 years ago

Around 3,000 years ago large cities emerged in some parts of the world. In Greece independent city-states formed. During this period empires such as the Persian and Roman empires emerged. The age of iron was born with the mining and manufacture of iron for tools.

At the same time, in Egypt, education began to be systematized. Education thus became more formalized and theoretical. The first schools were established.

1,000 years ago

During the medieval period the foundation of modern society and politics was laid. States and countries formed. Formal education and science flourished. Universities were established in Morocco, Italy, Egypt, Iran and England.

200 years ago

The Industrial Revolution occurred between 1760 and 1840. Important changes took place in manufacturing processes. Products which had been made by hand could now be made much more quickly by machines. New and faster forms of transport allowed increased movement of people and faster communication. The Industrial Revolution began in Great Britain and within a few decades had spread to Western Europe and the United States.

United States
Discovery

1844

Telegraphy - the sending of information along a copper wire - was invented in the 19th century. The first message sent by long distance telegraphy in America was transmitted in 1844 and read "What hath God wrought?"

1915

In 1915 the first USA coast-to-coast long-distance telephone call was made.

1928

The first regularly scheduled television service in the USA began in 1928 using only 48 horizontal lines of image. Today 2,160 lines are used in high definition television (4K HDTV).

1972

In 1972 the first personal computer (PC) was marketed.

1995

The Internet was available for commercial use for the first time in 1995.

2007

Touch screen mobile smart-phones were made available in 2007. Such phones had capacity for social networking, inter-continental communication, and eventually medical monitoring.

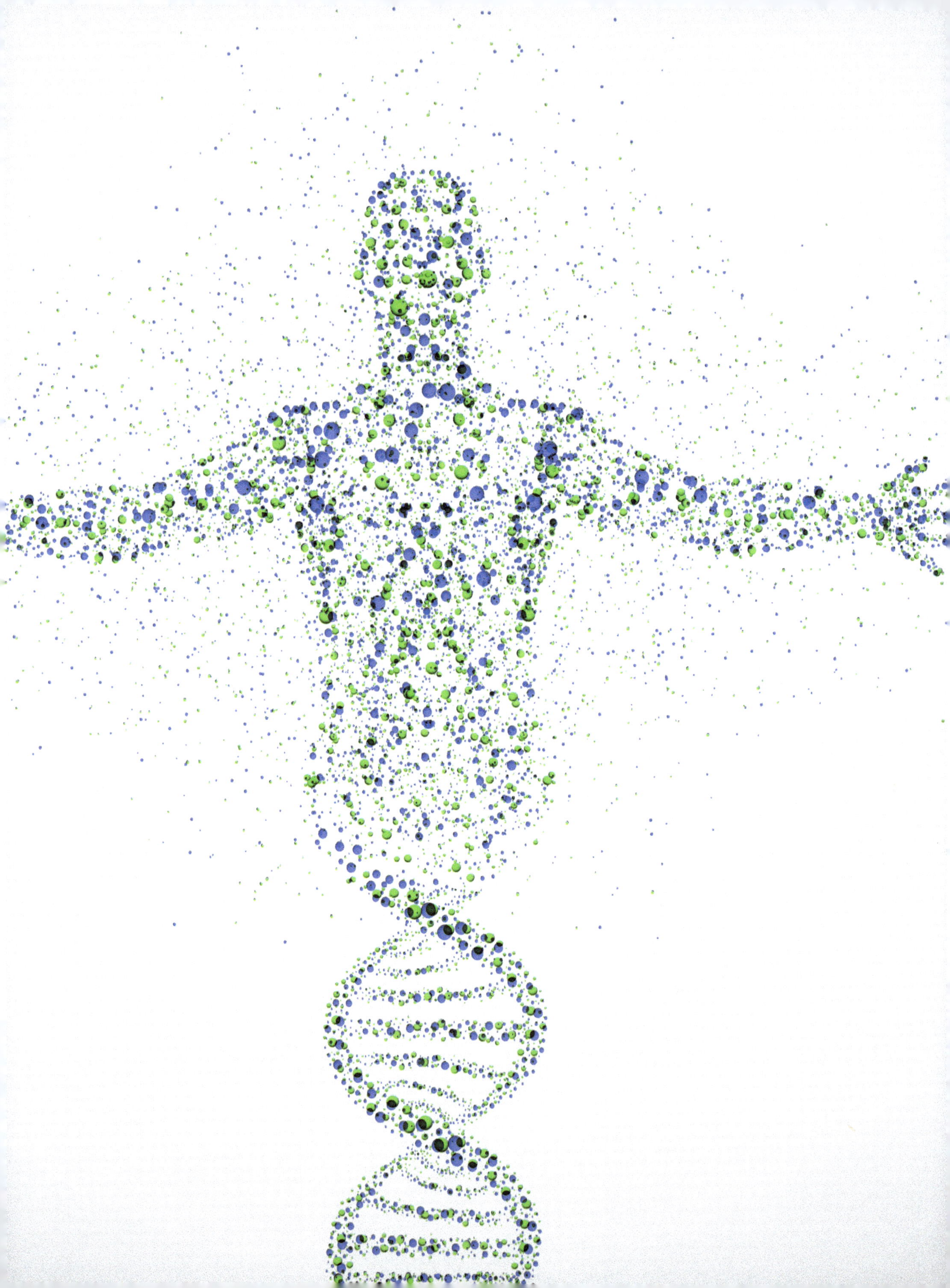

The above is a brief overview of the evolutionary processes leading to the emergence of the human being and society. At each stage of this evolutionary process latent properties emerged which were not at all evident in an earlier stage. For example...

The presence of hydrogen in the universe allowed for the formation of stars. As a result of fusion, light and heat were radiated, and the raw materials for planets were created.

Collections of elements lead to the emergence of essential proteins and amino acids which are the building blocks of all living things on Earth.

From the differentiation and organization of cells, algae, plants and trees emerged manifesting the latent capacity for photosynthesis. This process had the power to transform the atmosphere of Earth.

Also from the differentiation and organization of cells, there emerged what is now known as the nervous system and senses which, after millions of years of evolution, allowed for manifestation of the latent capacity of self awareness and consciousness in human beings.

From the organization of human beings into communities and societies, there may well be latent capacities which are emerging as human beings learn to operate and function cooperatively. As an organ is much more than the sum of its differentiated cells, societies made up of human beings working effectively together may reveal themselves to be much more powerful than the sum of the individuals of which they are constituted.

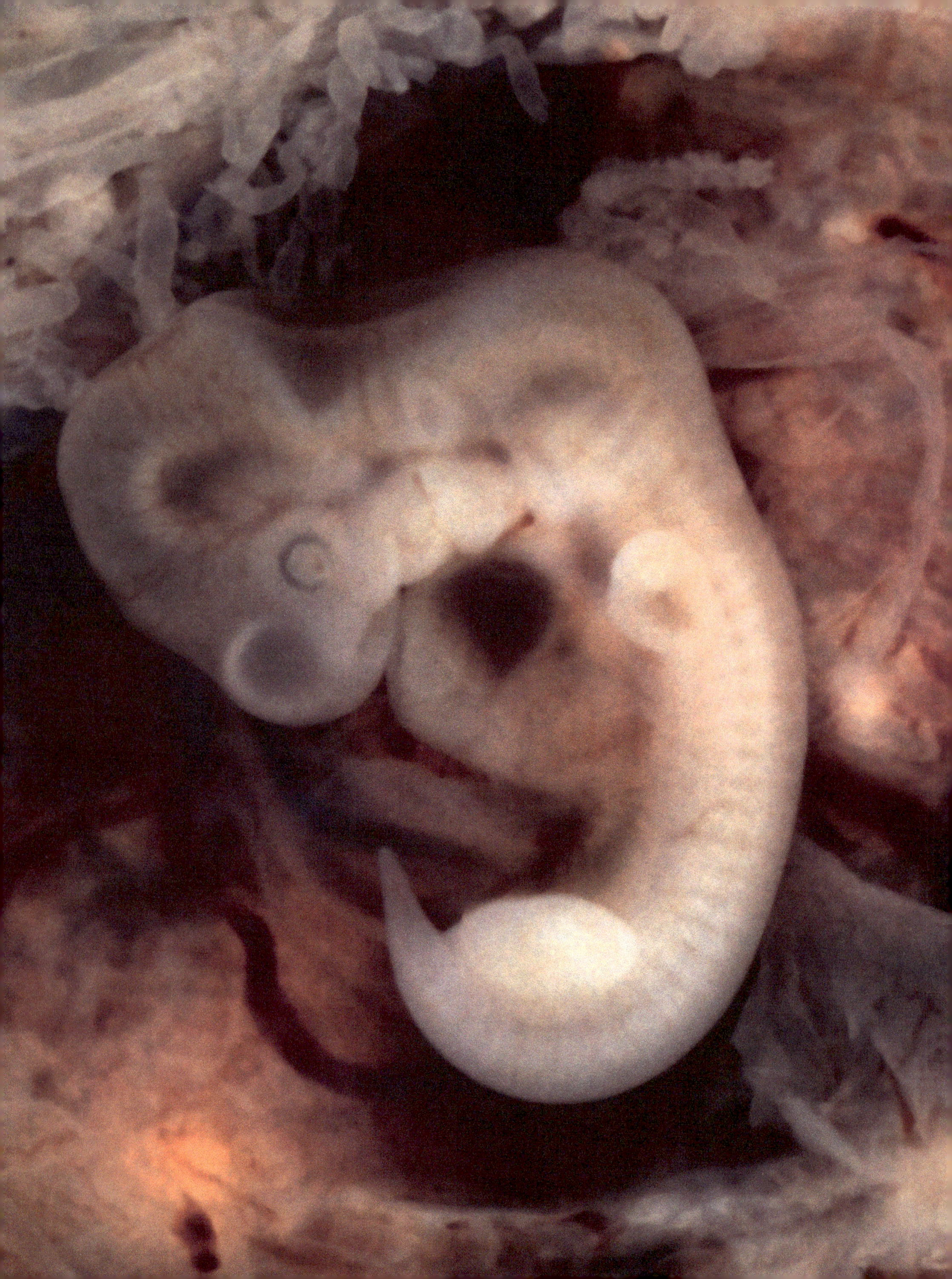

HUMAN BEINGS

The human embryo changes shape as it grows. Initially it looks like a worm, then gill slits develop and the body looks like that of a shrimp (reflecting the period when the highest point of evolution was a sea creature). Arms and legs bud and it looks like a salamander (reflecting the next stage of evolution which took place on the land). The skeleton forms and it becomes a vertebrate. Finally it takes on the form of a human baby ready for birth.

Just as the human embryo is destined to become a human being, Bahá'ís believe that the process of evolution was destined to culminate in the appearance of human beings. That is, evolution is not driven by chance and circumstance, but rather follows a predetermined plan towards consciousness. In its current stage the elements which are supported in the evolutionary processes are those that encourage unity with diversity, inter-dependence and social complexity, harmony, reciprocity, justice and equality.

This process is known as a teleological process - a process that is directed towards an end and has an intrinsic purpose. Just as the purpose of the embryo is to grow into a mature body, biological and social evolution have an underlying purpose.

Science Today

Using the tools of science, human beings are rapidly gaining knowledge of aspects of material existence. In some ways it seems science fully explains much about the material world. However knowledge, even of the material world, is limited. For example, light is referred to as 'perpendicular oscillating vibrations of electric and magnetic energy'. But what, in fact, does that mean? Mathematics describes it, experiments facilitate observation of it, and measurements allow comparisons but none of these tools actually identify the essential nature of light, nor explain why it exists.

Science seeks to offer some explanation of the "what" of material existence. It can describe the qualities and attributes of physical objects and relationships among them. It cannot, however, define the essence of even the simplest material entity, much less offer any satisfactory answers to the questions of "why?"

If we don't really know what energy is, or what matter is, then how can we define anything in material existence? Thus science is built upon assumptions or concepts of reasoning extracted from observation and prediction. This does not make science incorrect but merely identifies the validity of science within a range of known values.

In the study of the intangible, non-material, or spiritual aspects of reality, science' current understanding is limited.

Spiritual Reality

Quantum
vacuum
fluctuations

Humans
- consciousness

Material
Reality
(Spiritual Womb)

Atomic
particles

Animals
- senses & motion

Minerals
- attraction & repulsion

Plants
- growth

Physics has identified that all around us subatomic particles appear from nothingness and disappear into nothingness (known as quantum vacuum fluctuations). Currently science believes that something cannot come from nothing, yet this process occurs everywhere continuously. Perhaps empty space is not actually empty but full of potential?

Physics states that the speed of light cannot be exceeded, that it is intrinsic within the design of the universe; however, entangled photos of light separated by a large distance can switch their states simultaneously. Thus the communication of the change of state exceeds the speed of light.

What is this 'nothingness' from which subatomic particles come? What if entangled particles of light are actually connected through a non-physical dimension where the linear progress of time does not occur. What if everything in the material universe is interconnected through this non-physical dimension? Perhaps active forces within this non-physical dimension have the effect of creating the physical reality which we observe and experience? The nothingness or non-physical dimension has been given names like the ether and the void. It is also referred to as the spiritual realm.

Science has currently identified forces such as gravity, electromagnetism, and the nuclear forces, but there is another force which extends from the spiritual realm, the force of life. Unlike the other forces, life-force is not related to energy, nor is it material in nature. It is reflected through things of the material world. It is called spirit. Bahá'ís believe that it is this force which animates the material world, and that this force is fundamental to all life.

Spirit

The force which animates the material world is called spirit. Spirit manifests in increasing levels of complexity in minerals, plants, animals and humans.

The power or spirit of minerals manifests in the form of cohesion. Without cohesion there can be no minerals. At the next level, plants manifest the power of growth. This is the spirit of the plant. Organisms manifesting the animal spirit possess cohesion, the power of growth, and the power of the senses. Human beings, animated by the human spirit, manifest all the qualities above but also have the unique spiritual capacity called the power of the intellect.

Human beings are distinct from animals, just as animals are distinct from plants, and plants are distinct from minerals. The human being has never been an animal in its essence.[1] The human form evolved through the animal form. As the human form evolved it gradually matured to perfection, allowing a greater degree of spirit to become manifest.[2] At this stage the human form, animated by the uniquely human spirit, came into being.[3] The human spirit within the human form is also known as the soul.

Soul

The soul is a meta-physical (beyond physical) reality that cannot be perceived by our material senses. The soul is not made up of a combination of physical elements. It is not composed of atoms. All things that are composed of atoms must eventually decompose. The soul, however, does not decompose: it is immortal.

It is the soul that gives life to the human physical form, and what is commonly referred to as 'death' is in fact the separation of the soul from the physical form. The soul is also the source of the power of the intellect. It is the soul that gives human beings the capacity for rational thought, for intellectual investigation. It is the soul which allows human beings 'will' and free choice, which is denied in all lower forms of life. It is the soul which allows us the power to co-create our destiny and the world around us. It is also the soul that allows human beings to gain knowledge of the Animating Power, which guides the entire evolutionary process to its purposeful perfection.

The purpose of physical evolution is the perfection of the physical form. The purpose of the perfected physical form was to attract and house the human spirit, or soul. It is the soul which enters into a relationship with the Animating Power. This relationship is the purpose underlying physical and spiritual evolution. That is, this relationship is the purpose of creation.[4]

Manifestations of God

	Cycle of Fulfillment
Bahá'u'lláh	1863 CE. The Glory of God
Báb	1844 CE or 0 BE, approximately 200 years ago Start of Bahá'í calendar. The word Bàb means gate, the gateway to the Revelation of Bahá'u'lláh
	Cycle of Prophesy
Muhammad	622 CE or 0 AH, approximately 1,400 years ago Start of Islamic Hijra calendar
Jesus	0 CE, approximately 2,000 years ago Start of Christian calendar
Buddha	560 BCE, approximately 2,600 years ago in India
Zoroaster	1,000 BCE, approximately 3,000 years ago
Moses	1390 BCE, approximately 3,400 years ago
Abraham	1,800 BCE, approximately 3,800 years ago
Krishna	3,200 BCE, approximately 5,200 years ago in India
Adam	4,160 BCE, approximately 6,200 years ago

Note: Writings in the Holy Scriptures indicate the existence of minor Manifestations of God such as Noah (~2,700 BCE), Húd (~2,300 BCE), Sàlih (~1,600 BC) and others.

Example of year: If the date is 20 march 2014 CE (Current Era) in the Christian calendar, then it is equivalent to 1434 AH (Hijra year) in the Islamic calendar and 170 BE (Bahá'í Era) in the Bahá'í calendar.

MANIFESTATIONS OF GOD

The Animating Power of the universe (and beyond) can be referred to as the Creator or God. Throughout history the Creator has been called by many names - Allah, Yahweh, Jehovah and Great Spirit, to name a few. Whatever names or descriptions are attributed to the Creator are limited by the finite human mind. That is, God, in essence is unknowable and far greater than anything the human mind can conceptualize.

God is an unknowable essence, not human, not alien, not physical, not malicious, not manipulative but All-Loving, All-Forgiving and All-Knowing. In English the masculine pronoun, "He" is often used in reference to God but God has no gender. The use of "He" is due to a limitation of human language.

As God is unknowable directly, communication between the infinite Creator and finite human beings is made possible through the Manifestations of God, also known as Messengers or Prophets. These Manifestations have been sent throughout eternity, roughly once every five hundred to one thousand years, to guide humankind.

One Light
Many lamps

Bahá'u'lláh
(Bahá'í Faith)

Mohammad
(Islam)

Jesus
(Christianity)

God is One
All religions are one

Buddha
(Buddhism)

Moses
(Judaism)

Krishna
(Hinduism)

What are the Manifestations?

The Manifestations of God reflect the attributes of the divine into the human world. The guidance They bring causes spiritual and material progress.

God is likened to the sun - the source of physical life on earth. The Manifestations of God are like the rays of the sun. They bring the heat and light to earth (humanity) in a form that is accessible and not overwhelming.

Purpose of the Manifestations

The Manifestations of God have been sent down for the sole purpose of guiding humankind onto the Path of Truth. That is, the purpose underlying Their revelation is to foster material, human and spiritual education. The energy They release into the world is responsible for the progress of humanity. They provide the animating force through which the arts and wonders of the world are made manifest.

Many Messengers

Each Manifestation of God revealed the attributes and will of God, appropriate to the time in which He appeared. In this way, God gradually revealed more of Himself and His desire for humanity over thousands of years. This is known as Progressive Revelation. The Manifestations of God provide the most complete knowledge of God available to humanity at any given time. The differences among the various Manifestations of God and Their teachings, are due to the varying needs and capacities of the civilization in which they appeared, and not due to any differences in Their importance or inherent capacity. Their unity is absolute:

> There is no distinction whatsoever among the Bearers of My Message. They all have but one purpose; their secret is the same secret. To prefer one in honor to another, to exalt certain ones above the rest, is in no wise to be permitted.[5]

RELIGION

The Manifestations of God have served as a living link between the infinite and unknowable Creator and the finite creation throughout time. These Manifestations have always brought, and will always bring, guidance to earth:

> This is the changeless Faith of God, eternal in the past, eternal in the future.[6]

Human beings have records from only the more recent Manifestations of God - such as Krishna, Buddha, Abraham, Moses, Jesus, Muhammad, the Báb and Bahá'u'lláh. But undoubtedly Manifestations of God brought guidance to humans of which there is no longer any record, or of which there are only hints and traces of the original message.

The worship of the "life spirit" in animals, plants and other parts of nature - known as animism - is one example of this. The records of the original message from the Manifestation of God from many millennia ago are no longer available. Over time this message has come to take the form of stories, rituals and ceremonies that focus on the natural world and the intrinsic animating qualities of plants and animals.

Similarly myths and legends that speak of various 'gods' and 'goddesses' - such as Zeus, Aphrodite, Hades, Venus, and Jupiter - constitute distorted traces of past messages from previous Manifestations of God. The original message served as guidance for the people of time long past and this message has then been altered over time and is now passed on in the form of dramatic stories of deities interacting with each other and the human world.

The Manifestations of God from more recent times have also had Their messages distorted by human beings at times, for example when messages of love and brotherhood were corrupted by religious leaders to wage brutal wars and torture and kill people of other faiths. However, as there are some written records of Their guidance, the current understanding of the more recent messages is closer to the original intent of the Manifestations of God.

The guidance a parent gives a child changes over time as the child grows and enters new stages. However, throughout the changes and stages, the parent communicates love to the child and helps the child to foster healthy relationships with the parent and with others. So too, the messages of the Manifestations vary according to the time in human history in which they are revealed, but have constant and common threads that cross all periods. For example, each of the Manifestations of God has reiterated what is now known as The Golden Rule, as quoted below.

Krishna

Krishna provided guidance for the period beginning 4,000 years ago. His guidance provides the foundation for what is now called Hinduism.

> This is the sum of duty; do naught onto others what you would not have them do unto you.[7]

Moses

Abraham provided guidance for the period beginning 3,800 years ago. His teachings paved the way for the appearance of Moses. Moses provided guidance for the period beginning 3,400 years ago. His guidance provides the foundation for what is now called Judaism.

> Do to no one what you yourself dislike.[8]

Buddha

Buddha provided guidance for the period beginning 2,600 years ago. His guidance provides the foundation for what is now called Buddhism.

> Hurt not others in ways that you yourself would find hurtful.[9]

Christ

Jesus the Christ provided guidance for the period beginning 2,000 years ago. His guidance laid the foundation for what is now called Christianity.

> You shall love your neighbor as yourself.[10]

Muhammad

Muhammad provided guidance for the period beginning 1,400 years ago. His guidance provides the foundation for what is now called Islam.

> No one of you is a believer until he desires for his brother that which he desires for himself.[11]

Bahá'u'lláh

The Báb and Bahá'u'lláh provide guidance for the current period of humanity's history, starting in 1844. Their guidance provides the foundation for what is called the Bahá'í Faith.

> Blessed is he who preferreth his brother before himself.[12]

Shrine of the Báb, Mount Carmel, Israel.

Fulfillment

The Manifestations of God have always promised a time in the future when, the transformative processes to which they have contributed, will achieve fulfillment. That is, these processes will culminate in the appearance of a Manifestation of God whose message will unite the whole of humanity. Bahá'u'lláh is the Manifestation of God prophesied by the Manifestations of the past.

> I am not the first Buddha Who came upon this earth, nor shall I be the last. In due time another Buddha will arise in the world, a Holy One, a supremely enlightened One, endowed with wisdom in conduct, auspicious, knowing the universe, an incomparable leader of men, a Master of angels and mortals. He will reveal to you the same eternal truths which I have taught you. He will preach to you His religion, glorious in its origin, glorious at the climax and glorious at the goal, in spirit and in the letter. He will proclaim a religious life, wholly perfect and pure, such as I now proclaim.[13] (Buddha)

> I have many things to say unto you, but ye cannot bear them now. Howbeit, when He the Spirit of truth is come, He will guide you unto all truth...[14] (Christ)

> Whenever there is a decline in righteousness, o Bharat, and the rise of irreligion, it is then that I send forth My spirit. For the salvation of the good, the destruction of the evil-doers, and for firmly establishing righteousness, I manifest myself from age to age.[15] (Krishna)

Progressive Revelation

Each Manifestation of God is a channel for the revelation of God's Word and will to humanity. The revelation is primarily a release of divine energy into the world, allowing further material and spiritual progress. This divine energy is partially expressed in words. These words when written constitute the Holy Scriptures. Some of these are now referred to as the Bhagavad-Gita, the Torah, the Gospels, the Qur'an, and the writings of the Báb and Bahá'u'lláh.

These words serve as a guide and an impetus for progress for the period following their revelation. Immediately after the revelation of a given Manifestation of God humanity enters a divine springtime. This is a time of rapid spiritual and material progress which culminates in a collective divine summer. Over time the potency of the word is reduced and humanity enters into a time of stagnation or spiritual autumn, culminating in the degeneration of human morals and systems, similar to a spiritual winter.

It is at this point in the cycle that the next Manifestation of God appears, bringing a renewal of the divine revelation. Each time the word of God is renewed it contains elements specific to the period for which it is revealed, as well as reiterating eternal spiritual principles.

The goal and purpose of all revelation from God across the ages has been to provide divine education. This allows human beings to know and love God. Through the creation of an ever-widening circle of unity it also allows for the contribution to an ever-advancing civilization.

Humanity has passed through collective stages of infancy, childhood and early adolescence. It is now in the tumultuous period of adolescence, rapidly approaching adulthood. One of the signs of humanity's adulthood will be the unification of the entire human race. The earth will be seen as one country, and humankind as its citizens. Therefore the revelation of the Manifestation of God for today brought the guidance required to attain this state.

> The greatest bestowal of God to man is the capacity to attain human virtues. Therefore, the teachings of religion must be reformed and renewed because past teachings are not suitable for the present time.[16]

SPIRITUAL GROWTH

God has never and will never leave his creation without guidance. That is His promise to humanity. Human beings have the responsibility to strive to apply this guidance to their individual and collective lives. By applying the guidance brought from God to humanity by the Manifestations of God, human beings are enabled to grow spiritually. Though physical growth is mostly involuntary, spiritual growth depends on conscious effort.

> Without action nothing in the material world can be accomplished, neither can words unaided advance a man in the spiritual Kingdom. It is not through lip-service only that the elect of God have attained to holiness, but by patient lives of active service they have brought light into the world.[17]

A human being spends nine months in the womb in preparation for birth into the physical world beyond the womb. During that nine-month period, the fetus acquires the physical limbs and organs necessary for existence in this world. Though there is nothing to see in the womb, the fetus develops eyes, for eyes will be needed after birth. Though there is no need for limbs in the womb, the limbs develop in preparation for life beyond the womb.

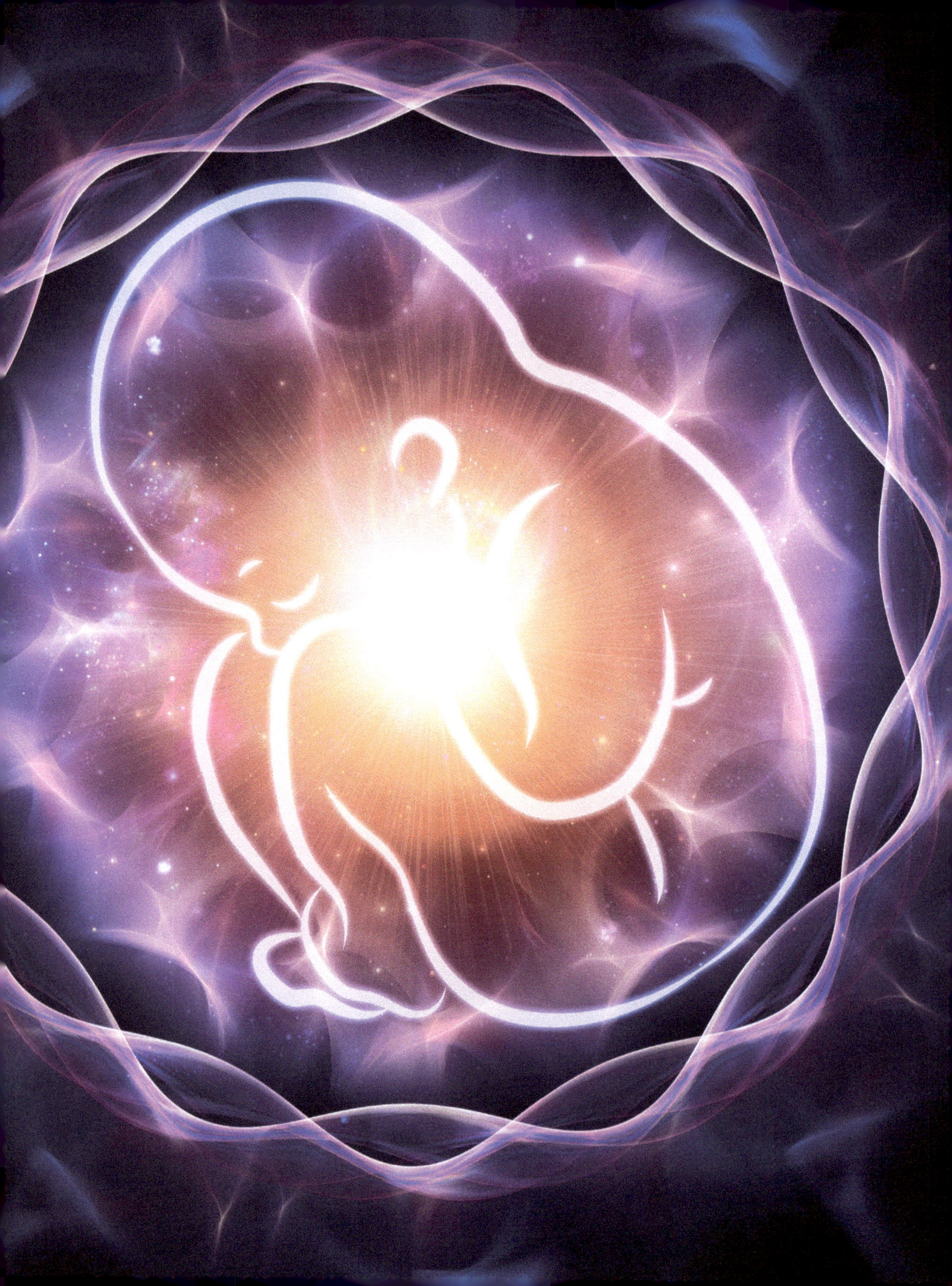

Similarly, the period of time a human being spends in the material world is a time of preparation for the spiritual world beyond. That is, the material world is like a spiritual womb in which the human being must develop spiritual limbs and organs in preparation for life in the spiritual world.

The spiritual limbs and organs that a human being can develop during life on earth constitute spiritual qualities. These qualities are constantly refined as a human being strives to apply the teachings from God to situations and interactions throughout their earthly lifespan.

> To consider that after the death of the body the spirit perishes, is like imagining that a bird in a cage will be destroyed if the cage is broken, though the bird has nothing to fear from the destruction of the cage. Our body is like the cage, and the spirit is like the bird.[18]

One way of thinking about spiritual progress is to think of the soul passing through various stages

1. The commanding soul - at this stage the soul commands that attention be directed to the trivialities of this world, and is infatuated with ephemeral desires.

2. The blaming soul - at this stage the soul becomes aware of the depths of its degradation and of its remoteness from its true goal. It awakes to a perception of its state, is filled with regret and blames itself for the depths of perversity and error to which it has sunk.

3. The inspired soul - as it rises from its lowly condition, the soul comes to understand those things that kept it abased and those things which will lead to its elevation. It becomes averse to those things that perish and is inspired to incline towards those things that endure.

4. The assured soul - this is the stage at which the soul is in remembrance of its Lord and sees the signs of God in the creation. As a result it is assured in its faith, its turmoil and unrest is calmed, it has quenched its thirst, soothed its torment; it has changed its darkness to light and unloaded its burdens.

5. The accepting soul - reaches a station of submission and contentment, leaving behind its searching and neediness. It entrust its affairs to God and is content with whatever God may decree for it. This is a happiness which is not followed by sadness. There remains no will, no rest, no motion, no destiny nor any fate except in God.

6. The accepted soul - in this state all-encompassing blessings and mercy reach it. Insofar as it has risen and left behind its passions and accepted the decree of its Lord, it becomes accepted in the sight of God, and in its state of nothingness, it is approved by its Creator.

7. The perfect soul - here it is characterized by divine perfections and comprised of godly attributes. It thus becomes the focal point of inspiration and the dawning-place for the Divine effulgences.

8. The soul of the Kingdom of God - here the soul confirms in its reality the profession of Divine Unity and establishes in its essence the sign of detachment. It attains to everlasting life and eternal living. It takes pleasure from spiritual delights the like of which no mortal eye has seen nor any mortal ear heard.

9. The soul of the Realm of Divine Command - this is a station far above the understanding of the minds of men, for this station is created out of the elements of power, authority, sovereignty, omnipotence, and freedom and nothing that has limitations or pluralities has any resemblance to it. Here the soul becomes aware of the secrets of hidden and invisible realities. This is the ultimate goal in the world of creation.

Virtues

> Regard man as a mine rich in gems of inestimable value. Education can, alone, cause it to reveal its treasures, and enable mankind to benefit therefrom.[19]

These words of Bahá'u'lláh indicate that every human being is born with immense spiritual capacity. Every human being can potentially manifest each one of the attributes of God, also known as spiritual qualities or virtues. These spiritual gems may be hidden beneath the earth within the mine, but with effort and with spiritual education they can be brought to the surface and polished. The potential for refinement of these virtues is unlimited and can continue throughout a person's lifetime.

> Every imperfect soul is self-centered and thinks only of its own good. But as its thoughts expand a little it will begin to think of the welfare and comfort of its family. If its ideas still grow more, its concern will be the wellbeing of its fellow citizens: and if its ideas grow even further it will be thinking of the glory of its land and of its peoples. But when ideas and views reach the utmost degree of expansion and attain the stage of perfection, then will it be interested in the exaltation of humankind.[20]

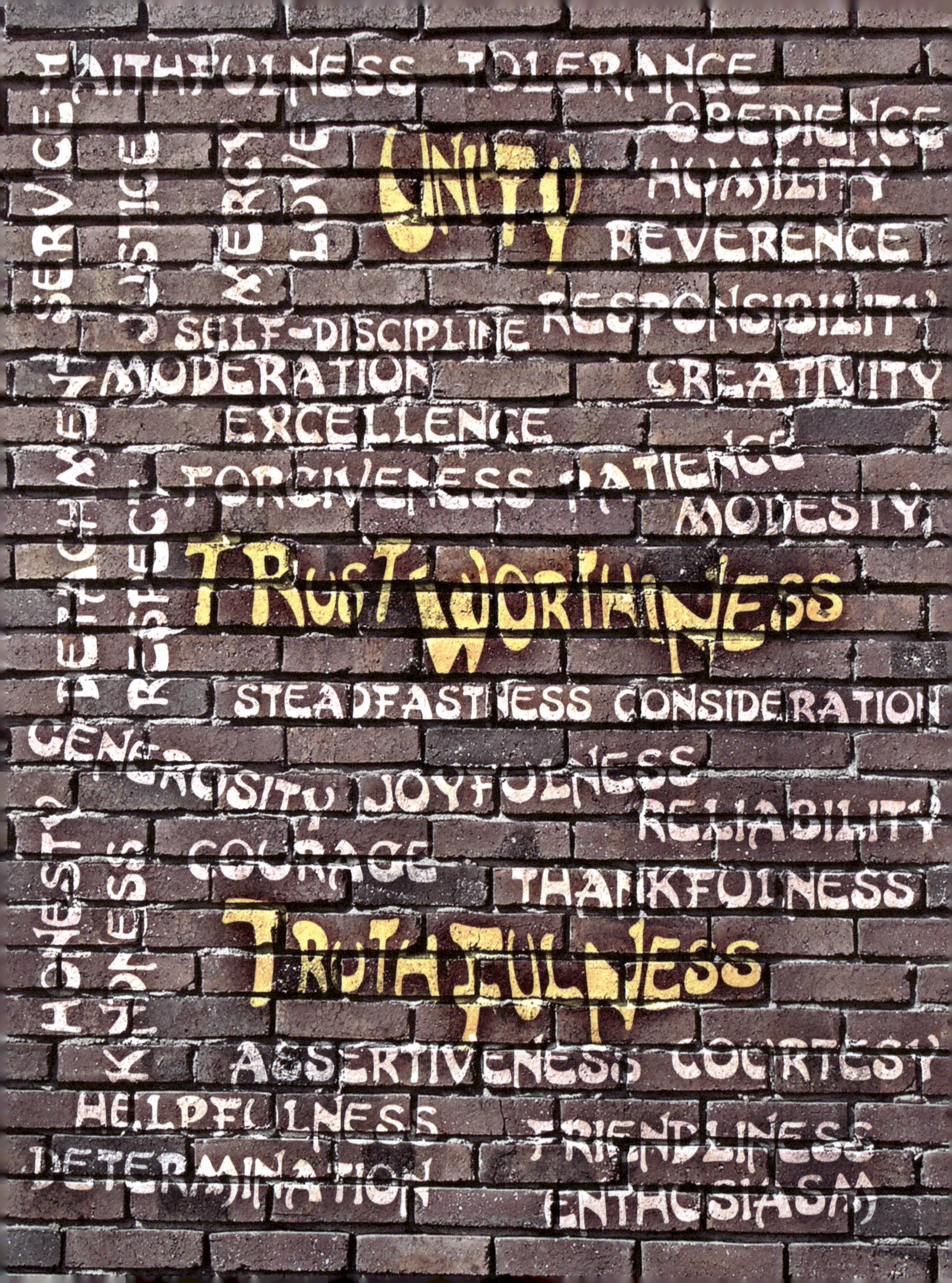

FAITHFULNESS
TOLERANCE
OBEDIENCE
SERVICE
JUSTICE
MERCY
LOVE
UNITY
HUMILITY
REVERENCE
RESPONSIBILITY
SELF-DISCIPLINE
MODERATION
CREATIVITY
EXCELLENCE
FORGIVENESS
PATIENCE
MODESTY
DETACHMENT
RESPECT
TRUSTWORTHINESS
STEADFASTNESS
CONSIDERATION
GENEROSITY
JOYFULNESS
RELIABILITY
HONESTY
KINDNESS
COURAGE
THANKFULNESS
TRUTHFULNESS
ASSERTIVENESS
COURTESY
HELPFULNESS
FRIENDLINESS
DETERMINATION
ENTHUSIASM

When the soul and the body part ways - often referred to as death - all that pertains to the body is lost. A person may be very physically beautiful, own a successful business, be outstanding on the sports field, or hugely popular and the life of the party, but at death these qualities will all cease to be. Virtues however, are eternal. These qualities of the soul transcend and continue beyond the disintegration of the physical form. They become the spiritual limbs and organs for the next stage of the soul's journey.

Transformation of Society

The power of the virtues is not, however, limited to the spiritual world, or to the life after death. Nor is it limited to impacting the individual. The development of spiritual qualities, or practice of the virtues, has the power to transform individuals, institutions and societies in the material world.

> The betterment of the world can be accomplished through pure and goodly deeds and through commendable and seemly conduct.[21]

If even just one of the virtues, such as truthfulness, was practiced by all people at all times, the impact on individuals, families, communities, institutions, and national and international relations, would be immense.

The development of *all* the virtues in individuals, communities and institutions of society, then, would make possible the realization of the following principles. These principles are the foundation of a world society, matured into adulthood. This is the guidance for today.

Principles for a New Society

Oneness of the human race

There is only one human race, diverse in color, language, and culture, but in essence it is one human family, inhabiting the planet Earth. That is, the human race is one human family bound together in a common destiny.

Equality of women and men

Full equality and a firm sense of partnership between women and men are essential to human progress and the transformation of society. Women and men have been and will always be equal in the sight of God.

Relinquishing of all prejudices

Prejudice, in its simplest form, is an erroneous preconceived judgment of others. It originates from a lack of awareness or from misinformation of the true character of people perceived as different from one's self. Relinquishing prejudice is necessary for peace and harmony among the people of the earth.

Universal House of Justice, Haifa, Israel.

Independent investigation of truth

One of the main sources of conflict in the world today is the blind and uncritical following of traditions, movements, and opinions. Independent investigation of truth requires the practice of honesty and justice, and an ability to see with one's own eyes and not through the eyes of others.

Spiritual solutions for economic problems

Extremes of wealth and poverty and other economic problems are rooted in qualities such as greed, corruption, and selfishness. They are not caused by a lack of resources. Thus the solution to these problems is also fundamentally rooted in spiritual qualities - such as fairness, equity, justice and honesty.

The harmony of science and religion

Science and religion are two windows or sources of information about one reality. Religion without science degenerates into superstition and fanaticism. Science without religion becomes the instrument of crass materialism.

2,600 years ago it was believed that the world was flat, and that one could sail off the edge.

Creative Evolution

Physics, chemistry, biology, and other branches of science all explore one reality. At times what is found in one may appear to contradict what is found in another. However, it is recognized that all the sciences explore one reality. It is therefore accepted that apparent contradictions are the result of temporary errors or inaccuracies in one or more areas, or in interpretation of findings.

Similarly, apparent contradictions between religion and science - which are both windows on one reality - can be recognized as temporary inconsistencies, limitations or misinterpretations of human beings. In essence, the two systems of science and of religion, reveal aspects of one reality and are fundamentally in agreement.

Prior to 1543 AD it was erroneously believed that Earth was the centre of the universe. Nine hundred years prior to this the Manifestation of God, Muhammad, taught that the Earth revolved around the sun. Thus for almost one millennium science and religion appeared to contradict one another but with time they came to agree. Similarly, the truths contained in the Revelation of Bahá'u'lláh are gradually being supported by knowledge revealed through science.

Over the past 13.8 billion years a divinely guided process has unfolded. It may have began with the 'Big Bang' - the release of immense energy. This energy then took different forms to allow the formation of stars and then planets. At least one of these planets, Earth, was hospitable and an environment evolved to sustain life. Minerals, plants, animals and humans evolved over billions of years in response to their inherent spiritual potential. This potential was instilled and guided by the Creator.

Simultaneous with the physical evolution of life on earth occurred spiritual evolution. This process was always and will always be guided by the Manifestations of God. In recent times these Manifestations of God have included Zoroaster, Krishna, Buddha, Abraham, Moses, Jesus, Muhammad, and the Báb.

The most recent Manifestation of God is Bahá'u'lláh. He brought guidance to take humanity to maturity or adulthood. It is now both possible and necessary for the human race to recognize its oneness and its relationship to the Creator.

Immense powers are now being released in the world as individuals and communities strive to align themselves with the spiritual guidance for today. There is a clear path before the human race to lead it to its spiritual destiny. Each person today has the bounty to choose to step onto that path, and walk toward the light. Each person has the opportunity to transform not only his or her self, but also his or her community.

Humankind must be a
lover of the light
no matter from what
lantern it may appear.

Humankind must be a
lover of the rose
no matter in what soil it
may be growing.

Humankind must be a
seeker of the truth
no matter from what
source it comes.

TRANSFORMING SOCIETY

The revelation of Bahá'u'lláh has provided the divine energy and the guidance required to achieve a united human race characterized by justice, honesty, and peace. The process of turning this energy and guidance into practical lines of action is a long and gradual one. People of vision and insight around the world are now engaged in consultation, study, action, and reflection to identify ways in which the Revelation of Bahá'u'lláh can be channeled to have its transforming effect.

At the moment this is taking the form of a spiritual educational process. This process consists of three parts which foster insights and capacities for service with children, junior youth, and youth and adults. This process is taking place all over the world. From the remotest African village to the Himalayas to New York City. Thus for a person of any age, in any location, wishing to participate in the transformation of themselves and their society there are clear avenues and opportunities for engagement.

HUMILITY
ARROGANCE
FAITH
HONESTY
RESPECT
FORGIVENESS
JUSTICE
UNTRUST-
WORTHY
STEADFAST
PATIENCE
TV
LAZINESS
COURAGE
$
UNITY
GREED
LOVE

Bahá'í Children's Classes

The first stage in the spiritual educational process is for children aged five to eleven years. These classes nurture the tender hearts and minds of children. Children engage with the Word of God, develop their understanding and practice of the gems or virtues within them. They learn of their own inherent nobility and dignity and of the nobility and dignity of all human beings. Through prayer and memorization, storytelling, art, drama, songs and games, they internalize the values and understandings that will allow them to contribute to a united, just and peaceful world.

> The education and training of children is among the most meritorious acts of humankind and draweth down the grace and favor of the All-Merciful, for education is the indispensable foundation of all human excellence and alloweth man to work his way to the heights of abiding glory.[22]

The teaching of these classes provide opportunity to junior youth, youth and adults to offer valuable service to their community. This service is transformative for the teacher as much as it is for the students.

Unity
Service
Social
Study
EXPLORING REALITY & ANALYSING SOCIETY
Truthfulness
BUILDING COHESIVE COMMUNITY
Humility
SPIRIT OF SERVICE
Respect
POWER OF EXPRESSION
Trustworthiness
TRANSFORMATION OF SOCIETY & INDIVIDUAL
Love
REINFORCE INTEGRITY & VALUES
Compassion
FRAMEWORK FOR DECISION MAKING
Honesty
PRINCIPLED & NOBLE CHARACTER
Courage
INHERENT ALTRUISM & JUSTICE
Justice

Junior Youth Spiritual Empowerment

The next stage of the educational process is for junior youth, aged 12-14 years. Junior youth have the opportunity to participate in the Junior Youth Spiritual Empowerment Program. This is a three year program which assists with the successful transition from childhood to adolescence. Its two-fold moral purpose is the transformation and spiritual empowerment of the participants and, through them, the transformation and unification of the community.

This program instills in the junior youth a keen sense of purpose, a commitment to spiritual and material education, a desire to undertake social action for the improvement of their communities, and the ability to resist the destructive and prejudicial forces within their societies. The junior youth come to understand that they are agents of change and have power to contribute to the construction of a better world. They are assisted to recognize the moral issues underlying everyday decisions and identify the moral implications of speech and action.

The Junior Youth Spiritual Empowerment Program is animated (facilitated) by youth mentors, many of whom have been through the program themselves. Thus this program provides opportunity for youth and adults to provide a valuable service.

Reflections on the Life of the Spirit

Ruhi Institute

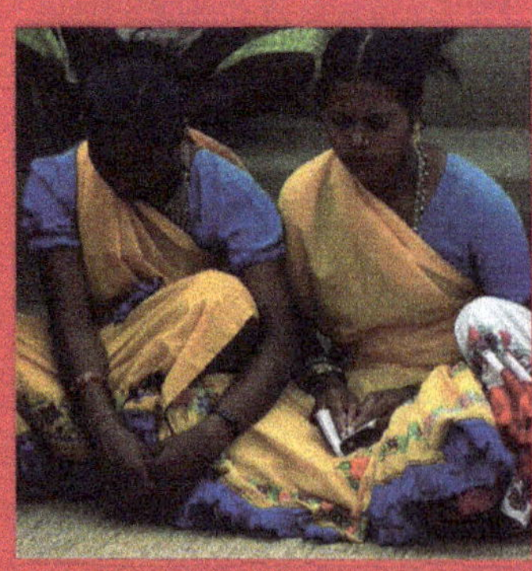

Book 1

Ruhi Institute Courses for Youth & Adults

The third stage of the educational process builds capacity in youth and adults for service. Youth and adults participate in a sequence of courses that foster spiritual qualities, insight, and practical skills.

As they progress through the sequence of courses participants engage with more and more complex acts of service, effecting transformation in themselves and their communities. Stage by stage, participants learn to understand their spiritual nobility, engage in meaningful and uplifting conversations, teach spiritual education classes for children, recognize that crises and victories contribute to personal and collective growth, and animate junior youth groups.

There is a gradually accumulating body of evidence that this model for the creation of a unified, just and peaceful society may prove effective. There are indications that its power is more lasting and profound than alternative approaches for which there is often advocacy such as changing a political party, changing a political system, increasing funding to a variety of narrowly focused projects or programs or agencies.

These opportunities to participate are open to every child, junior youth, youth or adult who would like to be part of building a better world.

Further research and information can be found at the
Institute for Studies in Global Prosperity

www.globalprosperity.org

Further information about the principles of the
Bahá'i Faith can be found at

www.bahai.org

[Science], the power of investigating and discovering the verities of the universe, the means by which man finds a pathway to God.[23]

"Science is the first emanation from God toward man. All created beings embody the potentiality of material perfection, but the power of intellectual investigation and scientific acquisition is a higher virtue specialized to man alone. Other beings and organisms are deprived of this potentiality and attainment. God has created or deposited this love of reality in man. The development and progress of a nation is according to the measure and degree of that nation's scientific attainments. Through this means, its greatness is continually increased and day by day the welfare and prosperity of its people are assured.

All blessings are divine in origin but none can be compared with this power of intellectual investigation and research which is an eternal gift producing fruits of unending delight. Man is ever partaking of these fruits. All other blessings are temporary; this is an everlasting possession. Even sovereignty has its limitations and overthrow; this is a kingship and dominion which none may usurp or destroy. Briefly; it is an eternal blessing and divine bestowal, the supreme gift of God to man. Therefore you should put forward your most earnest efforts toward the acquisition of sciences and arts. The greater your attainment, the higher your standard in the divine purpose. The man of science is perceiving and endowed with vision whereas he who is ignorant and neglectful of this development is blind. The investigating mind is attentive, alive; the mind callous and indifferent is deaf and dead. A scientific man is a true index and representative of humanity, for through processes of inductive reasoning and research he is informed of all that appertains to humanity, its status, conditions and happenings. He studies the human body politic, understands social problems and weaves the web and texture of civilization. In fact, science may be likened to a mirror wherein the infinite forms and images of existing things are revealed and reflected. It is the very foundation of all individual and national development. Without this basis of investigation, development is impossible. Therefore seek with diligent endeavor the knowledge and attainment of all that lies within the power of this wonderful bestowal."

- 'Abdu'l-Bahá, *Foundations of World Unity* p60, pre 1921

Michelangela

website - www.michelangela.com.au
email - info@michelangela.com.au

To receive Michelangela's occasional
product announcements
please visit our website to subscribe.

Unity in Diversity

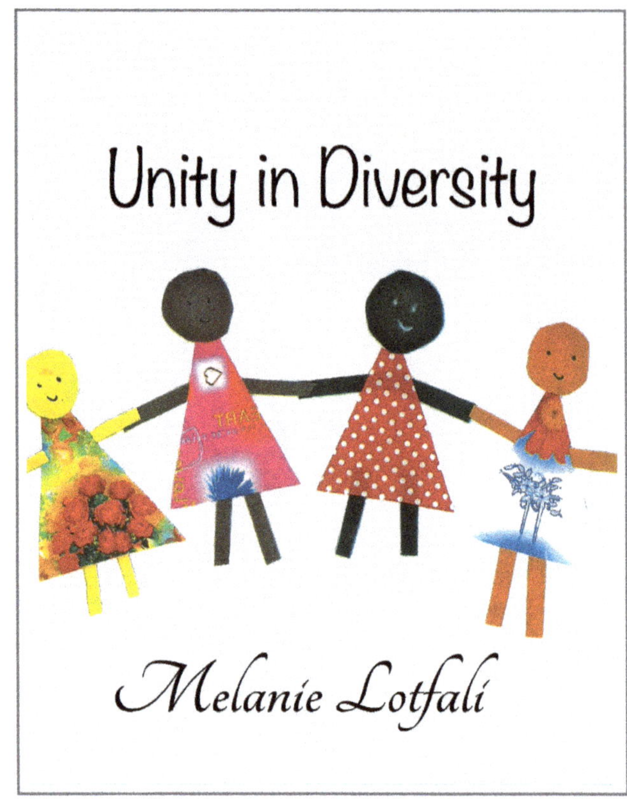

This brightly illustrated picture book contains five simple stories for young readers. They foster an understanding of the oneness of the human race and celebrate its diversity within that unity.

Likening the human race to various colored cotton in a woven cloth, various fruits on the tree of life, stars in the heavens, members of one body, and different notes in one perfect chord, the stories use the concrete to teach the abstract.

Young readers will enjoy the bright colors and simple text as they develop their understanding of the unity and diversity of the human race.

Ideal for children aged 4-8 years.

Order online from print-on-demand services, and digitally from the iBookstore. Also available as read-to-me stories in English, from the iBookstore.

Translated into French, Portuguese, Romanian, Tetum, and Mongolian.

Fellowship Farm

Leezah, Skye-Maree and Olingah Fitzgerald live with their parents on Fellowship Farm. In the first book of the *Fellowship Farm* series, you will meet the children and learn about their daily activities on the farm.

There is a lot to be done each day: pillow fights, morning prayers, pig feeding and school bus riding.They help their dad feed the cows, add stickers to their virtues poster and learn to deal with bullies.

Then you will join the Fitzgerald children on their many adventures with puppies, snake bites, treasure hunts, bonfires, camping by the sea, and tree houses. And as they go they sometimes practice their virtues, and sometimes forget...

Five volumes in the series, covering books 1-15.

Suitable for independent readers aged 8-12 years; parent-read from six years.

Order online from print-on-demand services, and digitally from the iBookstore or Kindle store.

The Divine Plan

This is the second book in the *Reflections on Reality* series.

Building on the foundation laid in the first book of the series, *The Divine Plan* examines social and cultural maturation throughout history.

The impetus provided by the Manifestations of God for this maturation is explored, as are the disintegrative and integrative forces at play in society today. It describes the opportunities, unique to this period of human history, available to the individual and the collective, to develop latent capacities essential to the establishment of a divine civilisation.

Suitable for independent readers aged 14+ years.

Order online from print-on-demand services, and digitally from the iBookstore.

Crowned Heart

The *Crowned Heart* series is the popular and inspiring collection of stories for young readers, drawn from Lights of Fortitude. It introduces three beloved heroines of the Faith.

"How many queens of the world have laid down their heads on a pillow of dust and disappeared... Not so the handmaids who ministered at the Threshold of God; these have shone forth like glittering stars in the skies of ancient glory, shedding their splendors across all the reaches of time." - `Abdu'l-Bahá.

These are the stories of Hand of the Cause of God, Martha Root, Clara Dunn and Corrine True. These easy to read stories are accompanied by truly exquisite watercolor illustrations by Katayoun Mottahedin.

Enjoyable reading for children 4-8 years of age.

Order online from print-on-demand services, and digitally from the iBookstore.

Dr Melanie Lotfali

Author of the *Fellowship Farm* series, *Crowned Heart* series, and *Unity in Diversity* series.

Melanie Lotfali PhD is a graduate of the Australian College of Journalism in Professional Writing for Children. She is the author of twenty-plus books of fiction and non-fiction for children, and the illustrator of five.

Melanie has taught spiritual education classes for children for the past twenty years in five countries and is currently an active animator and trainer of animators for the Junior Youth Spiritual Empowerment Program. She is a qualified counselor and classroom teacher, and for the past six years has facilitated violence prevention and respectful relationships programs in high schools.

Much of her childhood was spent on the farms, beaches, and mountains of Tasmania, where the Fellowship Farm series is set. As an adult, she spent four years in Siberia and four years in East Timor as a pioneer.

She currently lives in Lismore, Australia, with her family.

Michael Cohen

Author of the *Reflections on Reality* series and publisher of Michelangela's books.

Michael Cohen graduated as a Computer Systems Engineer in 1990 and worked for many years in software design and information systems. He changed careers in 2008 to become a Registered Nurse working in the area of Mental Health and Alcohol & Other Drugs.

Michael has been a keen participant in and advocate of the programs offered by The Foundation for the Application and Teaching of the Sciences (FUNDAEC) and Institute for Studies in Global Prosperity (ISGP).

He strives to contribute to processes and discourses leading to the progress of humankind toward a world society characterized by unity, justice and equity. A fundamental premise of Michael's worldview is that true science and true religion are necessarily in harmony, indeed are two windows on one reality. His writing seeks to promote understanding of this liberating concept and to contribute to a civilization that is ever advancing materially and spiritually.

He currently lives in Lismore, Australia, with his family.

Image Bibliography

Cover - Galaxy image © Space Telescope Science Institute - www.hubblesite.org
p08 Big Bang © Michelangela. Galaxy image © Space Telescope Science Institute - www.hubblesite.org
p10 Universe timeline - © Michelangela
p12 Galaxy © Space Telescope Science Institute - www.hubblesite.org
p14 Earth Cross-section © Kelvin Song - WikiMedia Commons
p16 Earth © Andrew Z. Colvin - WikiMedia Commons
p17 Solar System © Andrew Z. Colvin - WikiMedia Commons
p18 Local cluster © Andrew Z. Colvin - WikiMedia Commons
p19 Galaxy © Andrew Z. Colvin - WikiMedia Commons
p20 Local Galactic Group © Andrew Z. Colvin - WikiMedia Commons
p21 Virgo Supercluster © Andrew Z. Colvin - WikiMedia Commons
p22 Local Superclusters © Andrew Z. Colvin - WikiMedia Commons
p23 Observable Universe © Andrew Z. Colvin - WikiMedia Commons
p24 Water drop © José Manuel Suárez - WikiMedia Commons
p26 Cell structure - stock photo
p28 Evolution Chart © 2008 Leonard Eisenberg. All rights reserved. - www.evogeneao.com
p30 Evolution Spiral © United States Geological Survey - WikiMedia Commons
p32 Evolution of Plants © Michelangela
p34 Evolution of Mammals © Michelangela
p36 Evolution of Humans © Michelangela
p38 Village in Ourika valley, Morocco © WikiMedia Commons
p40 Bison painting in the cave of Altamira © Ramessos - WikiMedia Commons
p42 Accountancy Tablet © Jacques de Morgan, 1907 - WikiMedia Commons
p44 Child Labour © Lewis Hine 1909 - WikiMedia Commons
p46 Space Shuttle Discovery take-off 2008 © NASA - WikiMedia Commons
p48 DNA Man - stock photo
p50 Prenatal foetus (7 weeks) © Ed Uthman - WikiMedia Commons
p52 Simulation of Black Hole © Alain Riazuelo - WikiMedia Commons
p54 Spiritual Reality © Michelangela
p56 Spirit of a leaf © Michelangela
P58 Soul of a human-being © Michelangela
p60 Table of Manifestations of God
p62 Progressive Revelation © Michelangela, idea from Bahá'í literature
p64 Abstract Sun - stock photo
p66 Zimbabwian traditional healer © Hans Hillewaert - WikiMedia commons
p68 Neptune (Poseidon) © Erechtheus - WikiMedia Commons
p70 Buddha at Andhra Pradesh, India © Purshi - WikiMedia Commons
p72 Christ in stained glass © Alfred Handel - WikiMedia Commons
p74 Shrine of the Báb, Israel © Melody Ayeli. Melodrama ... on Flickr
p76 Holy Book - stock photo
p78 Mandala - stock image
p80 Prayer - stock photo
p82 Spiritual birth - stock photo
p84 Chakras - stock photo
p86 Opal © Hannes Grobe - WikiMedia Commons
p88 Kindness graffiti © Michelangela
p90 World hands - stock photo
p92 Universal House of Justice, Israel © Tom Habibi - WikiMedia Commons
p94 Flat Earth © Michelangela. Space image © Space Telescope Science Institute - www.hubblesite.org
p96 Big Bang © Michelangela. Galaxy image © Space Telescope Science Institute - www.hubblesite.org
p98 Lotus - stock photo
p102 World Flags © WikiMedia Commons
p104 Virtues Game. Created by Terry Turner.
p106 JYSEP © Michelangela
p108 Ruhi book 1 © Ruhi Institute

References

1 [M]an, from the beginning of his existence in the matrix of the world, is also a distinct species—that is, man—and has gradually evolved from one form to another.
'Abdu'l-Bahá, Accessed 13 December 2013 from: http://reference.bahai.org/en/t/c/FWU/fwu-19.html

2 [W]hen these existing elements are gathered together according to the natural order, and with perfect strength, they become a magnet for the spirit, and the spirit will become manifest in them with all its perfections.
'Abdu'l-Bahá, Accessed 13 December 2013 from: http://reference.bahai.org/en/t/c/BWF/bwf-26.html

3 [T]he perfection which you now see in man ... with regard to their atoms, members or powers—is due to the composition of the elements, to their measure, to their balance, to the mode of their combination, and to mutual influence . When all these are gathered together, then man exists.
'Abdu'l-Bahá, Accessed 13 December 2013 from: http://reference.bahai.org/en/t/c/BWF/bwf-21.html

4 If man did not exist, the universe would be without result, for the object of existence is the appearance of the perfections of God.
'Abdu'l-Bahá, Accessed 13 December 2013 from: http://reference.bahai.org/en/t/ab/SAQ/saq-50.html

5 Bahá'u'lláh, Accessed 13 December 2013 from: http://reference.bahai.org/en/t/b/GWB/gwb-34.html

6 Bahá'u'lláh, Accessed 13 December 2013 from: http://reference.bahai.org/en/t/b/PB/pb-63.html

7 Accessed 13 December 2013 from: http://humanityhealing.org/who-we-are/the-golden-rule/

8 Accessed 13 December 2013 from: http://en.wikipedia.org/wiki/Golden_Rule

9 Accessed 13 December 2013 from: http://humanityhealing.org/who-we-are/the-golden-rule/

10 Accessed 13 December 2013 from: http://biblehub.com/mark/12-31.htm

11 Accessed 13 December 2013 from: http://humanityhealing.org/who-we-are/the-golden-rule/

12 Bahá'u'lláh, Accessed 13 December 2013 from: http://reference.bahai.org/en/t/b/TB/tb-7.html

13 Accessed 13 December 2013 from: http://www.iawwai.com/BuddhistProphecies.html

14 Accessed 13 December 2013 from: http://www.kingjamesbibleonline.org/John-16-12/

15 Accessed 13 December 2013 from: http://bahai-library.org/books/hinduism/ch4.htm

16 'Abdu'l-Bahá, Accessed 13 December 2013 from: http://reference.bahai.org/en/t/ab/PUP/pup-113.html

17 'Abdu'l-Bahá, Accessed 13 December 2013 from: http://reference.bahai.org/en/t/ab/PT/pt-26.html

18 'Abdu'l-Bahá Accessed 13 December 2013 from: http://reference.bahai.org/en/t/ab/SAQ/saq-61.html

19 Bahá'u'lláh, Accessed 13 December 2013 from: http://reference.bahai.org/en/t/b/GWB/gwb-122.html

20 'Abdu'l-Bahá Accessed 13 December 2013 from: http://reference.bahai.org/en/t/ab/SAB/sab-35.html

21 Bahá'u'lláh, Accessed 13 December 2013 from: http://reference.bahai.org/en/t/se/ADJ/adj-2.html

22 'Abdu'l-Bahá Accessed 13 December 2013 from: http://reference.bahai.org/en/t/c/BE/be-56.html

23 'Abdu'l-Bahá Accessed 13 December 2013 from: http://reference.bahai.org/en/t/ab/PUP/pup-20.html

9 Accessed 13 December 2013 from: http://humanityhealing.org/who-we-are/the-golden-rule/

10 Accessed 13 December 2013 from: http://biblehub.com/mark/12-31.htm

11 Accessed 13 December 2013 from: http://humanityhealing.org/who-we-are/the-golden-rule/

12 Bahá'u'lláh, Accessed 13 December 2013 from: http://reference.bahai.org/en/t/b/TB/tb-7.html

13 Accessed 13 December 2013 from: http://www.iawwai.com/BuddhistProphecies.html

14 Accessed 13 December 2013 from: http://www.kingjamesbibleonline.org/John-16-12/

15 Accessed 13 December 2013 from: http://bahai-library.org/books/hinduism/ch4.htm

16 'Abdu'l-Bahá, Accessed 13 December 2013 from: http://reference.bahai.org/en/t/ab/PUP/pup-113.html

17 'Abdu'l-Bahá, Accessed 13 December 2013 from: http://reference.bahai.org/en/t/ab/PT/pt-26.html

18 'Abdu'l-Bahá Accessed 13 December 2013 from: http://reference.bahai.org/en/t/ab/SAQ/saq-61.html

19 Bahá'u'lláh, Accessed 13 December 2013 from: http://reference.bahai.org/en/t/b/GWB/gwb-122.html

20 'Abdu'l-Bahá Accessed 13 December 2013 from: http://reference.bahai.org/en/t/ab/SAB/sab-35.html

21 Bahá'u'lláh, Accessed 13 December 2013 from: http://reference.bahai.org/en/t/se/ADJ/adj-2.html

22 'Abdu'l-Bahá Accessed 13 December 2013 from: http://reference.bahai.org/en/t/c/BE/be-56.html

23 'Abdu'l-Bahá Accessed 13 December 2013 from: http://reference.bahai.org/en/t/ab/PUP/pup-20.html

www.ingramcontent.com/pod-product-compliance
Lightning Source LLC
Chambersburg PA
CBHW051559030426
42334CB00031B/3260

* 9 7 8 0 9 8 7 4 9 3 4 1 5 *